SMALL CHANGES, BIG RESULTS

SMART SKILLS FOR SMALL AND MEDIUM SIZED
BUSINESSES TO GROW AN AWESOMELY SUCCESSFUL
COMMERCIAL ENTERPRISE.

ANDREW JOHNSTON

NEW ZEALAND BUSINESS DEVELOPMENT LTD

National Library of New Zealand Cataloguing-in-Publication Data
Johnston, Andrew,
Small Changes, BIG Results
New Zealand Business Development Ltd
Email: admin@smallchangesbigresults.global

Book Layout ©2017 BookDesignTemplates.com

ISBN 978-0-473-44191-3

Contents

ACKNOWLEDGEMENTS

I have so many global connections that I could probably fill a book with people who have generously helped me on my journey so far, so please don't feel left out if you're not on the very short list below – your contribution has been genuinely appreciated.

My family - for putting up with me and my ambitious projects (business and personal) and supporting me as a tight family unit. And for putting up with my endless scribblings on our newspapers, ('The ramblings of a genius' as I like to label them).

New Zealander Bruce Wilson - for his encouragement, support, patience and cajoling as I ventured from employee to self-employed all those years ago.

Brad Sugars - for creating undoubtedly the best business coaching system in the world. If it wasn't for ActionCOACH business coaching, the systems and the phenomenal ActionCOACH community I wouldn't have helped hundreds of business owners across the planet from a small city in NZ.

Global Nomad Taki Moore - for showing me how to do it all with humility, style, and to a world-class standard. Dude, you're extremely clever and genuinely passionate about helping people. Much gratitude.

Will Fulton - for the fun times and trouble you got me into, a guy with a big brain and mischievousness nature, we clicked from the first time we met. You've helped me achieve more, with more people, often exceeding what they were hoping for.

Alida Niehaus - A South African treasure who gets me and challenges me. Calls me on my Bulls#*t sometimes too.

Brett Odgers in Sydney and his 'No BS Book Writing Program'. Without Brett and his program, I would have struggled to publish, let alone published in a timeframe I never thought possible.

All my business clients; we've laughed and sometimes cried on the way to smashing a lot of goals. It's always a blast and I believe in every one of you. Thank you for choosing me to be your coach.

All my global business coach clients, truly passionate people looking to change the world by improving a few businesses at a time. Total troopers.

INTRODUCTION – MY STORY

My work and business story began in 1986, when fresh out of high school, I managed to secure a fitter/turner apprenticeship with the Mataura Paper Mill in Southland, New Zealand. Born of a farmer, and growing up in southern rural New Zealand, I was very unworldly but knew even back then that the people who seemed to have the most money seemed to have a farm or some kind of business, they didn't work for other people.

My plan in '86 was to complete my apprenticeship so I would have something to fall back on and then buy or build a business to secure my place in the business world but, somehow I got caught up in the engineering career path, of striving for more qualifications, better job and higher salary. At twenty-three I sat my Third-Class Steam exams and become the youngest shift Engineer Supervisor in New Zealand, a few years later through a combination of distance learning and Central Institute of Technology block courses, I procured my New Zealand Certificate in Engineering in Power and Plant. Fascinated by steam turbines, hydro-electric plants and steam boilers I travelled to the UK and worked for four years in a smorgasbord of contract engineering jobs, accumulating in positions with Alfa Laval and Tetra Pak servicing their London buildings with heating, cooling and ventilation with beautiful little fire tube boilers. I set up a company (my first business!) and invoiced my employers each week to receive my pay packet. This business thing was a breeze.

Fast forward to 1995 and I was now back in New Zealand working for the southern hemisphere dairy giant Fonterra, but, starting to get bored with engineering, and my heart wasn't in it, so I started looking for something more interesting. I was attracted to a three-day property investing course a couple of young Aucklanders were running in the National Bank Stadium in Auckland, so a friend and I invested what seemed like a lot of money at the time to attend and learn. Life changing was probably an understatement... not only did we learn a ton about why and how to accumulate wealth though bricks and mortar but more importantly we also observed how these guys ran the event. It was such an amazing business model, a cheap venue dressed up with black drop sheets, black table cloths, a few banners and excellent lighting and sound, about seventy volunteers from previous events doing all the grunt work and then financial kickback alliances with developers, brokers, rental management companies and anything else deemed to be associated with providing a service to newbie property investors. Five-hundred people in the room at three-thousand dollars each, a low overhead model and then backend kickbacks, well, you do the math.

And full disclosure; there were parts of it that didn't sit well with me, things they told the audience they could do to gain properties, the rush to the back of the room selling, and a few other dubious practices, but the mindset change for myself and my friend was incredible. At one stage they had a live feed on two large screens of a young Australian, Brad Sugars, who spoke for about ninety minutes on property investing and also building businesses. This was the starting point for my interest in buying and building businesses and from that point on I started devouring books and audio (this was before the days of YouTube and fast internet access) on building businesses.

My first experience of a true business was a childcare centre that my wife and I built inside a decommissioned Catholic church. We converted the building and grounds with mostly our own hard labour into probably one of the nicest early childhood centres around at the time.

We built it so quickly and received our license from the Ministry of Education with virtually no hassles, I ended up doing an interview on TV about it. I remember being interviewed sitting on the decking with a microphone under my nose while a floor sander was grinding away in the background, I was confidently saying 'We'll be open in two weeks'. It was actually four weeks I think, but still a pretty good effort.

That business taught us a lot about financials, staffing ratios, minimizing expenditure, recruitment, systems, building team and business culture and many other aspects of business that you really only learn once you've actually jumped from the high board.

Even today I believe you have to finish building the plane once it's in the air, as there are too many unforeseen challenges to cover every contingency of buying or building your own business. That said, I also believe far too many business owners (particularly New Zealanders), jump into a business without doing enough, or any research, and without enough streetwise knowledge of how to run it so it doesn't become a liability. But more about that later in the 'Mindset' chapter of this book.

A few years later and I'm now working a full-time engineering position, running a full-time profitable childcare centre employing nine staff, plus three other profitable businesses in different industries, so what would be the logical thing to do? Quit my job and launch into full time entrepreneur nirvana you say? Well I could have, but the piece of me that had an employee mindset was holding fast to the concept of a steady pay-check, superannuation accumulation, and a pressed ham every Christmas from my employer.

Then, after building and buying businesses for about six years I thought 'Maybe I can be doing things in my businesses a lot better'? So, I engaged with a business coach from ActionCOACH Business Coaching. He came and met with me around our dining table, looked at all the profit and loss sheets, the balance sheets and business plans and goals I had, and finally said "You don't actually realize how well you're doing this, most business owners aren't doing a third of what you're doing. You should probably come and join our group of business coaches and teach what you know".

My initial reaction was "No way, I couldn't do that". However, over a period of several months, I thought about what he had said, and so, my next journey began. As it was a new business in a different industry to what I'd previously mastered, I did conduct a huge amount of due diligence before buying, and the New Zealand Master license holder told me later that no one else had been as thorough as I had.

I knew a lot of streetwise ways of building and growing businesses before I trained as a business coach, but I had never put a system to my approach, so armed with what is probably the best system in the world from the company that created the business coaching industry, I started to work with other local business owners. What an amazing and enlightening opportunity. I quickly accumulated many clients and many solid results in profits, sales, systems, team culture and so on, and before I knew it, in under a year, I was one of the top coaches in the world and people from other countries were asking me for advice.

In 2006, I very nervously spoke at a conference in Rotorua and received a standing ovation. Then, before long I had more invitations to speak, in firstly Australia, then America and Canada, then after a couple more years, multi-day trainings in countries such as South Africa, France, Ireland, Vietnam, China, Saudi Arabia and Columbia. Speaking though translators has been a steep learning experience but I've found that mostly business is conducted in the same way throughout the world, with the same frustrations and challenges. I've also found that the sense of humour in people is very similar no matter where you go. The last few years I've been travelling the world conducting a lot of business coach training, support and development across a thousand plus business coaches. Remember the young Aussie guy Brad Sugars I watched at the event in a live stream years ago? I even ended up contracting to him, to help develop business coaches in USA/Canada and Australia/NZ.

Over the years many of my friends and colleagues have encouraged me to write a book about my streetwise knowledge of building businesses and also the adventures I've had so far. This book is for all those that have encouraged me; and for all the business owners I haven't had the pleasure of shaking hands with yet.

May this book be a way of improving your business, your life and bringing us together so we can both be parts of each other's adventures.

[1]

THE CONCEPTS OF 'SMALL CHANGES = BIG RESULTS' — AND HOW THIS BOOK WILL HELP YOU

I have the privilege of many business owners around the world, contacting me asking to assist them in fixing, improving and growing their businesses, and I find in the initial conversations they are normally focused on increasing sales with the idea that more sales will equal more money in their back pocket. While that can be true, I have also found there is a ton of opportunity already existing in almost every business to increase the back-pocket quota before we focus on increasing sales and revenue. These gains are mostly simple, but you need to know where to look to find them, the devil being in the detail. Unfortunately, most business owners avoid looking at those little details like a disgraced sun-glassed celebrity avoids the paparazzi.

Mostly, everyone in business wants more profit, it's one of the major reasons to own a business, right? Well, the difference in profitability within a few little details can be huge. Take for instance a small business with revenue of just $400,000 and a Gross Profit (GP — before indirect costs are taken out) of 30%.

If we were to look at a lot of little details in the business and improve things to increase the GP by 1%, that would equate to another $4,000 profit, or, 5% - $20,000 profit, 10% - $40,000 extra profit. And the numbers get even more exciting if it's a $1,000,000 revenue business. An extra 10% GP = $100,000 extra profit.

Wait a minute, you say, that's pretty hard to do, and wouldn't the business owner already have done it? Well, that's exactly why I've written this book – to explain that it's not urban myth, and no, most business owners haven't taken the time to dissect, analysis and improve all parts of their business, and, it's reasonably simple. Let's be clear right here, there is definitely work to do to make it happen, but it's always worthwhile.

The concept I'm talking about is not new and one of the names for it is, 'Divide to Multiply'. It essentially says that if you divide anything up into all the little parts that make the whole, work on improving each part as much as possible, and then put it all back together, the result will be a multiplied outcome.

2 + 2 can actually equal 5, 6, 7... or, lots more!

Think about competitive cycling or yacht racing or Formula 1, in fact any top sports team. Every one of them analyses in painful detail every aspect of the bike, boat, car or team member to get any possible gain, even 0.1% better in every way could be the difference between standing on top of the podium, or not.

Another concept that ties in directly here, is called the 'Power of Marginal Gains', and can be explained as 'the 1% margin for improvement in everything you do'. As you strive for a 1% gain in every single aspect of part of your business, and keep repeating the process, the gains start to become accumulative and compounding. See the top line of graph on the next page.

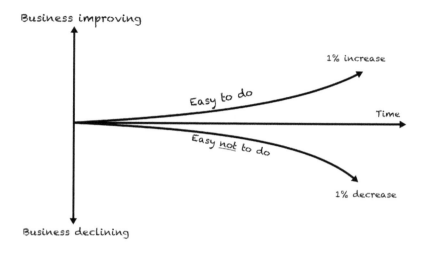

Inspiration for this image came from a graphic in 'The Slight Edge', by Jeff Olson.

But, there is also a dark side (there's always an opposing force, right?) And, it is also possible over time, for this concept to work in reverse to produce a worse result than what you started with. That is, if you constantly make bad adjustments or bad decisions, it will accumulate in an ever-increasing decrease in performance. In fact, if you do nothing at all in your business, this is also the consequence, because of ever increasing costs and expenses.

I often see this with a business that is in dire straits. The problems they are having wasn't one thing that happened last week, it's normally the sum of a whole bunch of slightly-off decisions or choices over a period of time.

A quick example is giving discounts to people in your business. A small negative thing in your business at the beginning, can lead to a BIG negative result. Discounting to a few customers at the start probably didn't matter too much, but continual discounting, combined with an increasing cost of the goods and increasing costs of running the business (wages, rent, insurance, freight etc.), start to make this a huge negative that can actually put you out of business. Notice the graph above; you can see in the beginning there is negligible difference, but over time the long-game result can be huge.

These concepts of divide and multiply and constantly striving for marginal gains, can be applied to every part of your business, from the GP on products, to your mindset and beliefs, to your marketing and sales systems, to team member performance, to accounts receivable, stock turn, financing, etc.

Now, let's use profits in a business as our sexy example; because everyone says they would like more profits, right? And, it is a primary reason to be, and stay, in business, to make profits so you can grow and achieve, help others, create employment and have a level of lifestyle you desire. Don't ever feel guilty about making a profit in your business.

A great friend of mine, Will Fulton, came up with a metaphor that really explains the effect of small changes = BIG results. If we think of all the opportunities to create more profit in your business as slices in a pie (a profit pie with profit slices), some opportunities will be large (maybe negotiating with a main supplier), some will be smaller slices (like reviewing the cost of your life insurance). We take a slice out individually and inspect it in detail for any improvements. Can we buy it cheaper? Can we price it higher? Can we build it faster? Can we sell less of it at the same price? Can we outsource it or part of it? Do we need it in the business? Can we make a small change/improvement to it?

When you've inspected that profit slice in every way possible and asked all the questions, you'll find in 95% of cases, an improvement can be made. We then put the slice back in the pie and move to the next one, repeating the process. Once we have gone through every profit opportunity in the profit pie, the profits will be accumulatively much more than when you started.

PROFIT SLICING

Inspiration for this image came from a friend of mine, Will Fulton.

Yes, a simple way to look at it, but please don't dismiss this concept as too simple. I have completed this process with businesses with revenue from $70,000 dollars to $70 million dollars and always found large gains.

While we are talking about increasing profits, I need to say that some profitability can be gained by reducing the expenditure down in a business, but, I have seen this taken to the extreme by some accountants and some business coaches. They try to drive down the expenses and, like squeezing a balloon, sometimes you can squeeze too far, and it can pop.

Most businesses can tidy up their expenditure, and it is one of the first things to examine. However, this strategy has limitations in that, you have to be careful not to be so brutal with reducing expenses that the business suffers. Not replacing the threadbare carpet in a reception area doesn't help the customer experience, not replacing the twelve-volt cordless drills with eighteen-volt ones that would speed up the carpenters' job, not freshening up the shop signage and repainting the peeling paint on the building, and so on, are all things that can affect the businesses revenue.

So, now you have an idea of the concepts that this book is based on, let's examine your beliefs and identity of being a business owner. You can have all the concepts and strategies in the world, but, if your belief systems and the identity of yourself as a business owner is poor, you won't implement and won't get the results you are truly capable of.

BELIEFS, IDENTITY, MINDSET AND DISCIPLINE

HOW IT ALL CHANGES WHEN YOU'VE HAD A CLOSE SHAVE

It hurt a lot. For a start, I thought I definitely had a tree branch imbedded somewhere in my forty-nine-year-old body. I couldn't breathe either, like I was winded but with each breath it wasn't getting better, in fact, it was getting worse, getting harder to breathe. I knew I had broken some bones too, I just wasn't sure where yet. I painfully turned from lying on my back to lying on my side to survey the damage, nope, nothing to see yet, no limbs at funny angles, no blood staining or leaking out, at least on my front side. But jeez does it hurt! By now my son Pieter and his friend Nic had arrived and the look on their faces told me the situation wasn't good.

The morning part of the motorcycle trail-ride had been going great, Pieter, Nic and I were riding fast and smooth, in fact Pieter had said at the last stop, "You're hauling Dad, I can't keep with you this morning", causing a smug smile inside my helmet, he is after all thirty-two years my junior. I pushed the button to make the blinky 'record' light start on the GoPro again and nailed the KTM's throttle. A rapid third gear burst down the bumpy fence line, 'That'll look good on video', and then a left turn and we're in the heavy forest again, single trail with enough mature pine trees to fill a ship bound for China, a couple of which I was about to meet up close and personal.

I've experienced a lot of high adrenaline activities in my life, but for me fast motorcycling is the bomb. It's pure and edgy with a high-risk element and most of the time I get it right, I push hard, and I don't get bitten. But, not on this Saturday morning. Not in this forest. Braking for the next righthand downhill corner would have been a good idea but instead I choose to give it too much gas at just the wrong time. Then the rear wheel stepped out of the rut to change the direction of the bike and now I'm looking down the barrel of some angry looking pine trees.

I don't really know how it happened in the next few seconds, but I do remember wrapping my back around one of those trees about a metre off the ground, then a hundred and twenty kilograms of KTM 350 hitting me, making a tree/Andrew/KTM sandwich, then the debris crashing to the ground in a pile of man and machine. Turns out the initial tree impact broke seven ribs (probably more but the doctors stopped counting), broke my back in two places, and also punctured my right lung. Then the bike hit me, and to add insult to the situation, also broke my knee and thumb.

I'll be clear here and say up front; it was my own fault (although I do like to say testosterone and the earths gravitational pull played a part), but I had to decide to put it behind me and carry on.

Ten days later I drove myself to my doctor. The conversation went like this: "So how many days ago did you do this to yourself"? "Ten". "You know you shouldn't have driven yourself here right"? "Oh"? "And I bet it hurt driving"? "Yeah it did a bit". "Andrew, do you realize how serious this accident was"? "Ummm, not really, but I'm guessing it now". "Honestly, that accident could have easily killed you, it was very serious, and you should know that you're very lucky to still be with us, if you had had one more little thing happen with your busted body at the time, or in the ambulance, or at the hospital you probably wouldn't be standing with me right now".

They say it sometimes takes a traumatic life event to change your prospective on life, to make you realize what's important and what's not, so for me this accident was huge, and it started a two-year path of reflection that has changed my beliefs and mindset, and, my direction forever.

Eighteen months later I was at a global business coach conference in Vancouver, Canada, and the speaker was encouraging everyone to set goals, dream bigger, strive to be more, do more and have more, and it got me thinking deeply about success. So, in the question section I stepped up to the mic and challenged the speaker. In front of two-hundred people.

My question was, "Is it ok to be content with where you are now and not bother with striving all the time"? He answered my question with a question (it's a room full of coaches, what did you expect?), which was "Well, what is success to you personally"? Inside I gritted my teeth and dug deep for an answer, then I relaxed and said. "Joy; from every moment, every minute in life, every interaction, joy from every achievement big or small".

I kind of surprised myself with the string of words, and I think up until the serious motorcycle accident I would have answered in a much more cliché way, like; 'Having enough money to have freedom, or bringing up a successful healthy brood of children, or giving back to the community, or having properties, toys, Lear jets and Lamborghini's' and all that stuff. But I had a changed perspective and kept (keep) thinking 'What the hell are we striving for? What are we chasing?' It's easy to get caught up in a misplaced faux sense of chasing what we believe is success and actually neglecting to recognize the constant moments of joy we can experience. It's a cliché of course, but 'Success is a journey, not just a destination' - it's actually true.

Do the Lamborghini's and Lear jets have a place? Yes of course, and I can tell you from personal experience Lamborghini's are a heap of fun to drive! And, I presume a Lear jet would be nice too. If you want to have that kind of lifestyle, then go for it! But, make sure you are experiencing joy in every moment along the journey rather than expecting joy at the other end when you've 'made it'.

> Note: I'm not saying you shouldn't set goals for your business and life and strive to achieve them. My message here is to encourage you to evaluate your current situation and work out how to achieve the maximum amount of pleasure or happiness, or joy, from everything you are doing in life <u>as</u> you strive for whatever you want to achieve.

IT ALL STARTS FROM BELIEF INDOCTRINATION

We form beliefs as we travel though life about how we should measure ourselves, on how we are doing, or how successful we are. One of the problems is, that these beliefs are formed from experiences and indoctrinations of parents, relatives, friends, peers, teachers, society, the government, TV, social media, marketing agencies, employers, workmates, etc. There are a ton of influences and often a simple throwaway comment from someone close to you can begin to mould a belief that either drives or deters you from a level of achievement or success in life. In fact, a simple comment can turn into a belief that completely sets a certain direction for your life. My parents were hugely supportive of me completing a trade apprenticeship because, 'You'll always have something to fall back on', so that belief took me down a path of engineering and employment. In this case, neither bad nor good, just a path.

There are also unfortunately, some belief indoctrinations that can be destructive. In mild forms they can cause a person to never really attain what they are capable of, or they can cause pattern behaviour, for example; getting into a relationship that is going well, then upsetting the situation so the relationship fails (sometimes called Repetitive Dysfunctional Relationship Patterns). In extreme form, negative beliefs can cause a life of crime and prison food.

I meet a lot of business people who are disappointed or upset where they are in life compared to where they thought they might be at this stage of their lives. They have slogged away for years and feel they haven't got a lot to show for it. They are normally tired and disillusioned with their business and thinking 'Maybe this is as good as it gets?'

When I reflect with them on what they have actually done so far and who they are becoming, it is truly a revelation, as the normal focus is on *how far they are,* from where they want to be, rather than, *how far they've come*. Often this is coupled with directly comparing themselves to other people's achievements, believing that their success should be measured this way.

Whoever you are, whatever you've achieved, (or think you haven't), here's my advice - stop being so dam hard on yourself and stop measuring yourself against others, it's your journey, your life, and it doesn't have to be like anyone else's. A good daily exercise to start feeling better, is to write down or state out loud each day, some things in your life you are grateful for. Small things, large things, things that you've previously taken for granted. As an example, when I walk out to the mailbox each morning I often say something like, 'I'm grateful I get to experience another sunrise, another day on this spinning planet'. Because as we all know, everyday there are many people who don't get to experience another day.

Here's a couple of redefining thoughts I've learnt over the years about beliefs:

- You *CAN* change your seemingly concrete set beliefs and therefore change your path from this moment forward. And, it doesn't have to take a traumatic event like a serious motorcycle accident for you to do this.

- The best *IS* yet to come! It doesn't matter if you're thirty, fifty or seventy years old, you have accumulated a lot of wisdom so far in your years on this earth. Imagine focusing fifty years of experiences and wisdom into your fifty-first year, especially once you have worked on some limiting core beliefs.

IMPROVE YOUR IDENTITY AND BELIEFS, IMPROVE YOUR BUSINESS

To be a business owner takes courage, more courage I think, than being an employee. There's more risk, more frustration, more financial commitment, and, there should be more rewards. In fact, proportionately many more rewards. Like the ability to take time off, the monetary rewards, and all the little perks like tax deductible conferences on a Fijian Island. And yet I see not only in NZ, but all around the world, business owners who don't have the business results they dreamed of and in most cases, deserve. Of course, they don't have the rewards they deserve either. In fact, some business owners don't even have it as good as some of their employees.

People say the formula for success is: **BE x DO = HAVE**. If you want to **HAVE** things in your life, like business success, financial achievements, successful relationships; in fact, achievement of any goal you set, then you need to **DO**, that is, you need to implement actions (preferably with a plan). But the other thing that needs to happen, is you need to mentally **BE**come the person who achieves these things, so you need to adopt the beliefs and identity of the person who is achieving, or will achieve, the **HAVE**s.

The mathematical base here also shows that you need to have large amounts of both *BE* and *DO* to achieve a large *HAVE* result.

BE x DO = HAVE.

1**(BE)** x 1000**(DO)** = 1000**(HAVE)**

 and 1000**(BE)** x 1**(DO)** = 1000**(HAVE)**

But... 1000**(BE)** x 1000**(DO)** = 1,000,000**(HAVE)**
- This result is a thousand times more than the first two equations.

This concept that beliefs can have an enormous effect, is far reaching, as it extends to anything you have achieved already and anything you will achieve in the future. If you are a good tennis player, you will have the beliefs, identity and confidence of a good tennis player, if you are good with business financials then you will have those beliefs and identity. Conversely, if you are always telling people 'I'm not good with names' then you will have the internal belief and identity of someone who isn't good with names. Or numbers. Or marketing. Or leadership. Or... Well, you get the drift.

The truth is that a business owner wears many hats, and has many identities, in fact the smaller the business is, the more identities the owner has to have, I guess you could say schizophrenia is alive and well in business owners!

Some of the identities most business owners need to adopt are:

Great at leading

Great at marketing

Great at sales

Great at delegation

Great at organizing self and others

Great at employee selection

Great at resolving problems

Great at analyzing financials

Great at making informed quick decisions

Great at negotiating

Great at reading people - employees and customers

Great at installing systems

Notice I haven't even mentioned 'Great at doing the business activity', in fact, most business owners I've met are already good, great or a guru when it comes to doing the activity that is the actual business. It's normally the reason they choose to go into business in the first place - they were already a great plumber as an employee and a business came up for sale, or they decided to buy a van, print business cards and launch into business for themselves. Many cafe owners were already passionate and great at baking, making coffee, and interacting with people.

So, looking at the sample list I quickly produced above, you are probably already pigeon-holing yourself into the things you are good at and the things you shy away from? Well, I have some good news for you, everything on that list and more can be learned. You just need to change your belief around that skill or ability, and then work away at developing that skillset. We don't come out of the womb as a great marketer or great at financials, we develop all our skills as we travel though life. Now it's understandable that we do tend to naturally like working on improving some skillsets and veer away from others, but to build and grow a business that doesn't hold you hostage you will need a diverse set of abilities, and some knowledge in *all* areas is required for a successful profitable enterprise.

There is also more information available to you at your keyboard than has ever been seen before in the history of humans engaging in business. Can you imagine how hard it was for a Roman era plumber to deep dive learn about financials? The challenge here is not what you need to learn, or where to go for the information, it's more about are you willing to work on your beliefs and identity and then go to work on the skills to learn it?

Exercise: Rate yourself from 1 -10 on the following business owner attributes:
1 being 'Yeah, I need to get better at that'
and 10 being 'I'm actually world class at that':

Leading ___
Managing ___
Marketing ___
Selling ___
Delegating ___
Organizing self and others ___
Employee selection ___
Resolving problems ___
Analyzing financials ___
Making informed quick decisions ___
Negotiating ___
Reading peoples personalities – both employees and customers ___
Building systems ___

Do You Actually LOVE Being a Business Owner?

CASE STUDY: MIKE THE BRICK GUY
(Note: Names and business types in the case study examples have been changed to protect identities).

Most people are capable of running, growing and enjoying life as a business owner, but occasionally I meet someone who just shouldn't be in that space. A few years ago, I was contacted by a guy manufacturing bricks, Mike had a little two-man factory, worked hard and sold quite a few bricks. Trouble was, when I investigated how it was going, he was trading insolvent and couldn't pay his bills. Nice guy, hard worker but wasn't making the right decisions. Why would that happen then? Well there were many business management problems but a major one stemmed from the liberal use of a barter card type system where he was trading pallets of bricks for points.

Under a microscope I found numbers like this: Quote for a load of bricks - $12,000 then take 50% in card points, so $6,000 points and $6,000 in money. Seems reasonably harmless so, far right? The problem was that the Cost of Goods on the $12,000 was $9,000 so in essence the $12,000 job was losing $3,000. This might have worked if he could have brought raw materials or paid expenses with the card points but (at the time at least) the options to redeem the card points were very limited, in fact he had already used a bunch of points on fishing and hunting equipment for personal hobby use.

After this had been going on for a couple of years the situation was dire, personal guarantees had been signed and no matter which angle I looked at it, I couldn't find a way of helping him dig his way out. The short story is that the bank and finance companies closed him down, took all his equipment, his house, cars etc, and he was left with nothing.

I felt really bad for him, but I could see he wasn't really cut out for the business world.

Fast forward twelve months, I was at an organized motorcycle trail-ride with my sons and I heard my name called out, it was Mike, we chatted, and he told me he was happy (he actually looked younger) and he had secured a job on a dairy cow farm that paid well, supplied a house, meat for his freezer and fuel for his car, all as part of the job and he had no stresses of running a business. Great outcome and he was indeed a happy man. As you can see, occasionally it's a better option for a person to be gainfully employed than losing hair and sleep, trying to run a business.

However, don't despair if you're now reading this and wondering if you should be in business! The fact you are reading this book indicates to me that you're probably open to doing things differently in your business and getting better results than you've experienced so far.

The important thing in owning a business, is not to just love the product or service you're selling (although I have met a few that don't even love that anymore), but that you move towards loving every aspect of business, from marketing, selling, recruiting, leading, testing and measuring everything, putting systems in place and so on. It's like a career of learning and personal development, and it doesn't stop, there's no end to this journey. But if you decide to put your head in the sand, stop learning and think you know everything about business, then you'll be stuck, and you'll probably get left behind in some areas in the future.

YOUR PERSONAL DRIVERS

Let's talk about what drives your desires to improve your abilities as a business owner. Like an iceberg with only its top ten percent above the waterline, your customers, your staff, even your friends and family only see the small percentage of what's going on for you. They see your actions, your reactions, your decisions, your behaviors and your results, but people don't see what is below the waterline, your beliefs, values, identity and also the environment you put yourself in with friends, family, and time by yourself. Underneath the water, there is a lot going on. Remember it was the ninety percent of ice mass below the surface that sent the Titanic to Davy Jones Locker, not the ten percent above the surface.

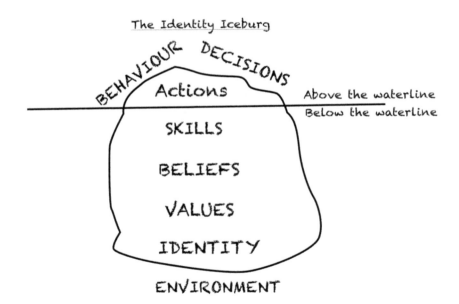

Starting at the bottom of the diagram, the **Environment** you put yourself in or let yourself be subjected to, is one of the big influences. The environment can determine what you are successful at in life and what you aren't and what you do or don't strive for.

And you can choose what your environment looks like. It may mean you need to spend a little less time with friends who are negative, speak badly of others, or are not interested in achieving much in life. It could be that you need to reduce your daily news intake through radio, TV and social media. Inherently bad news will get the attention of humans many times more than good news, many people say it's due to our internal fight or flight spidey senses. We want to know what is bad, 'Is it close to me? Do I need to fight or flee'?

Unfortunately, this subtle negative environment can have a serious effect on our minds, our wellbeing, our identity, and our values and belief systems. Have you noticed over the last ten years or so that there has been an increasing number of tragic events, foul language, gore, and complete programs dedicated to protecting ourselves from apocalyptic events, all extensively shown throughout viewing mediums including the internet, movies, games and TV shows? If you feed your mind with it (and you probably are without realizing it), I think you'd agree, it's all a bit depressing right?

The good news here, is that in most countries, you can choose what you watch, listen to and the people you associate with on a regular basis, but you do have to make a conscious effort to do so. *Your own environment shapes your identity and determines who you think you are or are not.*

A quick way of working out your **Identity** as a business owner is to write 'I am' and then whatever comes to mind to complete the sentence. Do this with as many 'I am' lines as possible until you have no more ideas and you will then start to realize what your identity looks like.

So, it could look like this:

I am very good with customers

I am a hard worker

I am very good at completing sales

I am good at organizing my team, etc.

Then you can also do the same for 'I am not', so the list could look like this:

I am not very good at marketing

I am not good at watching the financials

I am not recruiting good people

I am not good with my time management, etc.

If you find a few things in your identity you want to change, then congratulations, as **Different Identity = Different Results**. There have been plenty of books written on how to implement lasting change to your identity but a simple place to start is to write out 'I am' statements with the desirable attribute that you wish to have as a business owner.

Such as: I am fantastic at analyzing the financials and numbers in my business. Then say and write it a few times every morning and every evening. It will start to permeate your subconscious brain and you will notice you will become more interested in learning how to make this statement a reality, you'll ask different questions, you'll pick up books on the subject and you'll find your identity changing to match what you are programming your mind with.

Next up on the iceberg is **Values**. Values are normally shaped by significant people and circumstances as we grow up and are also very deep rooted. They are also principles held by all humanity. They can affect everything in your business and personal life, and have different ratings or emphasis put on them by each person. For example, if your parents didn't put much value on schooling, and perhaps English class in particular, then you may have grown up with a lack of vocabulary and understanding of more complicated words and sentences. This can lead to a disadvantage when reviewing, constructing or analyzing contracts and agreements with landlords, suppliers and staff. If you grew up working your first job with a business owner who was dishonest and didn't declare all the business revenue for tax purposes, then your values on declaring money for tax might be different to mine. Honesty is a value held in most cultures but how it is expressed may vary. In some countries they hold the value of honesty so high you might lose your hand if you are caught stealing.

Other values you may feel strongly for or against are:
Excellence
Integrity
Communication
Success
Contribution
Results, etc.

Next is **Beliefs**, these are beliefs that you currently hold to be true, they may or may not be actually true, but in your mind, they are true. 'It's hard to get good people', might be a belief you have, but it might not be true for the business owner down the road who has a belief that 'Good people are out there and it's straightforward to find them', and so he always finds good people to work in his business.

It's worth noting that a belief can be changed, in fact turned upside down very quickly if there is a traumatic or substantial event. What if your belief was 'There is no other intelligent lifeform anywhere else in the universe other than humans', and then an alien knocked on your door one night asking to use your Wi-Fi? Tongue in cheek example but you understand what I mean. Or how about your belief in Santa Claus being real? This belief is so strong for millions of children around the world that they write letters to the North Pole but stop immediately when they find out it is actually their parents buying and giving them presents at Christmas time. (Sorry if this has just shattered one of your own closely held beliefs)

The final thing that is under the waterline is your ***Skillset***. This may be very noticeable to others or it could be very subtle. The skill set of being a fantastic 'Lead from the front' type leader is very clear to others, whereas the quiet coaching type of leadership is very subtle. Both can be very skillful. A skill is normally 'An activity repeated until you reach unconscious competence'.

The way I work with my clients on the Identity Iceberg is I get them to choose a ***Behaviour*** they want to develop, such as planning ahead in their business. Then I challenge them on the ***Belief*** surrounding that behaviour, particularly the way they are doing or thinking about that business activity, note - this is usually contrary to their existing belief. Then I get them to develop one or more ***'I am' statements*** conducive to improving that belief, and hence, that behaviour. Next, I get them to choose ***Values*** they have around that behaviour and how that will relate to improving that behaviour. Then we look at the ***Skills,*** tools, training that they will need. And finally, ***Environmental*** factors that will help them stay on track to achieve the behavioral change.

HERE'S AN EXAMPLE: The behaviour the business owner wants to improve is 'Always planning ahead for the next day'. The Belief that drives this is 'My days are always a lot more effective when I plan ahead'. One of the Identity Statements could be 'I am an organized, disciplined and effective business owner, always planning ahead to maximize my results'. The Value that drives the belief could be 'Honest day's work'. The Skill the business owner wants developed is 'The discipline and focus to plan ahead at the end of each day'. The Environment that surrounds that person could be: associating with other business or sports people or friends that are disciplined and focused on their goals and results and getting them to hold accountable the business owner. They don't phone or text at 4.30 and say 'Hey forget the planning today, It'll wait, get down here, I have a beer waiting for you', because they respect the business owners planning time. Instead they ask, 'How did the planning go today?'

By putting some effort in and making small changes to each level of the Identity Iceberg, any business owner is able to produce BIG result changes on the surface, where everything is visible to others. Commit to implementing that behaviour as your improvement focus, and you will too.

ACTIVITY:

Commit to looking at your existing results, behaviors and actions and analyzing them to see if there are areas you would like to improve. Then dig deep on your identity, values, beliefs and skills around that behaviour. Lastly look at how you can change your environment to help you achieve the changes you would like.

"You will never change your life until you change something you do daily. The secret of your success is found in your daily routine". John C Maxwell

DISCIPLINE IS ESSENTIAL

When it comes to discipline, I have a concept called 'Pushing though the first few minutes'. This is something I realized a few years ago and I've been sharing it with clients and coaches ever since to help them change their mindset around a little short-term pain for huge long-term gains.

As an example, imagine you feel the need to improve your health, fitness or lose some weight and you have done some research and decided you need to run four times each week to achieve your goal.

Can anybody run? Yeah pretty much, it's one of the things that is genetically installed into us as humans, for instinctive dangerous animal fleeing and all that. Do we all want to run? Hmmm... well I've got to say personally, it's not my idea of an ideal start to the day. However, it may be for you. But, what can't be argued are the health benefits of cardiovascular fitness, muscle toning, weight loss, increased endorphin levels for happiness and so on. So, personally I do run, not because I'm a runner (far from it) but because I understand the short, medium and long-term benefits from it.

I needed to frame this running thing up with you in this way, so you understand I don't really want to run, and I'm not one of those guys who much prefers wearing dirty Nike's over a set of suede Maher's. What I have realized is that right after the run, I feel pretty good, my breathing is better, my lungs feel great, I have this nice little muscle burn going on, endorphins are flowing, and I feel like I've achieved something worthwhile. Actually, back it up fifteen minutes and I realize I also feel pretty good half way though the run, when the blood is pumping, my hearts pounding, I'm panting, and my muscles are working. It makes me feel good to be working my body as nature intended.

Time lapse back another fifteen minutes to the start of the run and I have to be honest, I'm hating it. My muscles are far from warm, they're actually hurting a little, my hearts protesting, and my mind is saying 'You clown, you could be still snuggled up in your warm bed'. In fact, if we go back a further five minutes to the moment the alarm went off, I had to consciously swing my legs out of bed, walk across the room and don my smelly running gear, I've got to say at that moment, it just isn't featuring on my bucket list.

So, the first few minutes of waking through to the first few minutes of running are not what I would call pleasant (for me at least - you might be different), but the benefits of completing a run four times per week are huge, in short term, medium and long term good wellbeing results.

All you need to do is push though that first few minutes of your mind, body and soul protesting.

Nowadays my question to myself with anything I don't want to do, learn or experience is, 'Am I going to let the first few minutes of pain or discomfort jeopardize the multiple benefits this will give me in short, medium and/or long term?' I have found I have achieved more than many of my friends, family and colleagues over the past few years with this simple question.

This is the question you could ask yourself about learning financials, marketing, sales, leadership, systems, time efficiency and anything else you know you are lacking expertise in to improve your business and life. They say, 'Everything you truly want is outside your comfort zone, otherwise you'd already have it'. I think starting and pushing though the initial stages of anything you need to learn that will wildly benefit you, is a comfort zone breaking quest.

KEEP LEARNING, LEARNING, LEARNING

Many people seem to think that once they leave school their education is over, and they don't have to worry about learning anymore. Understandable I guess, as for a lot of people school probably wasn't the greatest experience for them, and sometimes it's hard to see where the learnings of $y = e$ to the power of x or the synopsis of 'Lord of the Flies' fits into a business career. But having a mindset that you are always willing to learn and develop yourself, will actually drive you towards the top five percent of business owners out there.

I've been to many trainings, workshops and seminars, where people who have achieved greatness in a field are speaking about their path to success, what they did, what mistakes they made and how they pushed though. I chat with people in the audience at the break and they shrug their shoulders and say 'Yeah, I've heard all that before, nothing new', or worse, 'Yeah, but what he didn't mention was all the failures he's had'. My adage is always 'If I learn one new thing from this person then my time has been well invested', and often I can turn that one learning into hundreds or thousands of dollars or more for my own or my clients' businesses.

I hope I can encourage you to take a mature attitude and adopt a lifelong love of listening, learning and personal development. And congratulations on picking up this book, it's a very good practical start to learning how to be a better business owner and run a better business.

[3]

WHAT'S YOUR TIME ON THIS EARTH WORTH AND HOW ARE YOU USING IT?

VALUING YOUR TIME

Every human on this incredible planet was born with an equal amount of time, twenty-four hours each day, or one-hundred and sixty-eight hours each week. We need to sleep approximately eight hours per night, eat and wash, dress, travel, drink coffee, for a minimum of two to three hours per day and then there is playing with the children, watching a bit of TV, checking Facebook, Pinterest and Instagram, leaving us around ten or eleven hours for working in and on our business. The point I want to make here, is not that we have limited time, but that we all have about the *same* time, and I know there are people in this world who do extraordinary things with that same amount of time.

Richard Branson runs over four-hundred companies (mostly from a hammock), in those same one-hundred and sixty-eight hours. The difference between people like Richard, and you and I, is that they have learned the value of their time and then learned how to leverage their time.

But I have good news! You too can most probably improve how you are spending or investing your time. But what's your time actually worth? Do you realize there are probably activities you are personally doing in your business that could be done by someone on minimum wage? And conversely there are activities that you can do in your business that will yield you hundreds or even thousands of dollars for minutes invested? Most New Zealand business owners don't stop to work this out and end up running around all week with their hair on fire, dealing with customers, staff and problems, just trying to make the ends meet.

Many Business owners also feel either guilty about taking time to work ON their business. Sometimes they feel their time is better spent working IN the business, servicing customers, answering the phone, doing the work rather than working ON the business making improvements and building systems. I'm here to shed the light on the fact that there is a better way.

THE FUN SKILL MATRIX

Helping and coaching you completely through that process is beyond the scope of this book, but I do want to introduce you to a simple tool to emphasis what your true hourly rate can be as a business owner. It's called 'The Fun/Skill Matrix' and it's one of the first tools I use with business owners to help them become many times more efficient with every hour they invest in their business.

See the diagram on the following page.

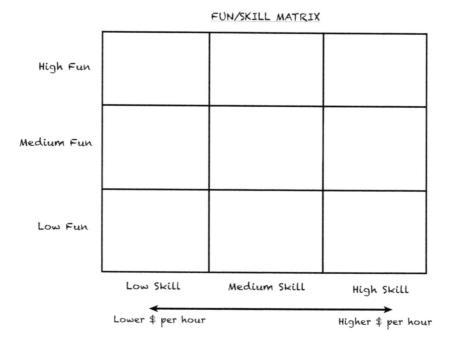

FUN/SKILL MATRIX

On the vertical axis we have **FUN** from low to high, this designates the activities or tasks you are doing in your business that you enjoy a lot and those that you detest doing. On the Horizontal axis we have the **SKILL** level required to do each task that you are currently completing hourly, weekly, monthly, even yearly, in your business.

Once all the actives or tasks are placed in the boxes we can see on the left side the tasks that you could pay a person with low skill and a low hourly rate (regardless of how much fun or how enjoyable those things are), and on the righthand side are the activities that require a very high skill level, some of which will yield you a lot of profit or cashflow for the business, often for only minutes of your time. E.g. following up on quotes and closing a sale is something that is high skill and high value to the business when executed successfully. Strategic planning, margin analysis, costing analysis are also examples that will need your skills and add high value to the business, because you will be able to make informed decisions regarding the profitability and growth of your business, in fact investing time working on your business like this will be worth thousands of dollars going forward. Running a business doesn't mean you need to run around making yourself busy doing everything (who said that was a badge of honor anyway?).

THE STORY OF THE LION, MICE AND ANTELOPE

It's interesting that a lion living on the African Plains can actually capture, kill and eat a field mouse. However, it turns out that the energy to do that is greater than the calorific content of the mouse. So, if a lion spent his whole day hunting and eating field mice, it would slowly starve itself to death.

A lion cannot live on mice. Lions need to eat antelopes. Antelopes are big. While they take more speed and strength to capture and kill, once killed, they provide a huge feast for a lion and its pride. A lion can live a long and happy life on a diet of antelope. The difference between mice and antelopes is really, really important relative to how the lion spends it time.

If in your business, you're spending all of your time and energy going after 'field mice', your short-term rewards are a feeling of activity and maybe even accomplishment. However, in the long run, your business will suffer, perhaps even die.

The questions to ask yourself are: Am I spending my day chasing mice or hunting antelope? Can I use my time better to focus on the bigger things in my business rather than the smaller, issues? What are the size of the clients that I am targeting for future growth of my business? 'Mice' type energy expending clients, or larger clients that will be more profitable, and take less energy. In my own Early Childhood Learning Centre business, the clients who had their children with our centre for twenty-five plus hours per week were always less hassle than those that dropped their children off for two hours per week. So, guess who I focused our marketing towards? Antelopes rather than energy hungry mice.

ANALYSING YOUR CUSTOMERS TO DETERMINE WHERE TO SPEND TIME

I often do an exercise with my clients where we analyze the customer database for the previous twelve months to ascertain which customers are buying from the business a lot, and which aren't. In most cases it will be an approximate split of 20% contributing to 80% of the revenue. Turns out that Italian Economist Vilfredo Pareto was right with his 80/20 theorem.

> For example, a specialist engineering company I worked with found that 76% (roughly $800,000) of their revenue was from 23% of their past twelve months customers, the remaining seventy seven percent of customers contributing approximately $250,000 of the revenue. The next step was analyzing what they were actually purchasing, which then lead us to target and market to that sector. Less time and effort for a bigger monetary result. Antelopes instead of mice.

[4]

THE 7 AREAS MONEY CAN 'DISAPPEAR' IN A BUSINESS

Over the last fifteen plus years, meeting with, and working one-to-one with business owners, a common statement I've heard again and again is: 'The accountant says we made $xxxx.xx money last year but I don't know where it is', usually followed by 'And he says because we made money, we have $xxxx.xx tax to pay?'

In reality it is possible to make an awesome profit on paper and then struggle to pay bills and taxes, but thankfully it is normally easy enough to find where the money is going or has gone. Then at least you can go to work to fix or minimize it happening in the future. The money is always in one or more of the following seven areas:

ACCOUNTS RECEIVABLE OR DEBTORS

If you are a business that invoices some or all of your products or services, then the nemesis of cashflow and profits can be customers (debtors) not paying on time. Many profitable businesses end up in a situation where they are technically trading insolvent due to not being paid on time by customers, which in turn means they are not able to pay their own bills when they fall due. This causes enormous stress on the business cashflow, the business owner, and usually the office accounts person as well.

There are several reasons why debtors can pay you late; here's seven of the most common I've found, read though these carefully and you'll then know where to start looking for solutions.

1. The Terms of trade are not strongly positioned or set with the client
2. The invoices are being processed and then late being sent out
3. The invoicing cycle is too long (instantly, or at the minimum, seven-day invoicing are the best practices)
4. The overdue debtors are left far too long before they are contacted
5. The debt collection system in the business is not good enough, hint: sending another invoice with an overdue stamp on it ain't going to do much
6. Communication isn't established when there is the first sign of a problem with an invoice
7. The invoice payment or part payment isn't negotiated when there is a payment problem

In some situations, an increase of business transactions and invoices going out may be stretching the cashflow. This is good and bad of course, more business (as long as it is profitable) is great, but more debtors not paying you, isn't much fun.

> **Factoring:** Factoring can be an option for some businesses, but I've always managed to avoid it by helping business owners tighten all the parts of their cashflow. Factoring is when you engage an outside company for collecting the money from your monthly debtors, the company pays you immediately, then goes to work getting the money in for themselves, they normally take a commission of around 10% so it's a substantial cost but you do get the other 90% of your money on time every month.

OVERSTOCKING

The next area that causes cashflow crunches for businesses is overstocking with goods or products, this is often caused by an overzealous employee doing the ordering or an overzealous salesperson saying, 'But if you buy xx amount, I can do it for a super-dooper deal of $xx'. I experienced this a lot with the supermarket I personally owned and sometimes found I had three months of a product line instead of one or two weeks. It ties your business cash up and also hampers your business for growth i.e. if you have an overdraft of say $40,000 and are constantly maxing it out with the latest low Gross Profit product deals, then if you wanted to double the business, in basic terms, the overdraft would need to double.

I'll talk about stock levels and stock turn later but a quick test to see if you are over stocked is to take a field trip around your business and point at anything that has dust on it. I did this once with a toy store owner and found lots of items that had two, three, or even five years of dust, meaning the initial money to buy those products was still sitting on the shelves (visualize each one of your products as a pile of money bills that should be in your cashflow). In the food industry you have the added complication of dated shelf life and also the cost of holding the stock may be high if it is a frozen or refrigerated product line due to the electricity costs.

In a motorcycle store many of the new motorbikes are on a 'floor plan', which means the owner is allowed to have the new motorbike displayed without paying for it and pay little or zero interest for thirty days, sixty days or even ninety days. BUT, after that time frame is up, the motorcycle needs to be paid for and is now costing interest to have sitting around. I've found It takes a lot to convince a motorcycle store owner to discount a model (back to cost price or less if necessary), to move it out the door, but if it's a slow-moving model, or worse, a newer model has superseded it, then it's time to take an axe to the price (or value add some accessories), to get that pile of money bills back where it can be used more fruitfully.

CAPITAL EXPENDITURE

One of the quiet profit and cashflow enemies of a business can be spending (or hopefully investing), for better/newer/bigger plant. This is a tricky balance as you normally need reliable, cheap to run and maintain equipment rather than old plant that lets you down, lets your customers down, and costs the equivalent of a small city to run and maintain. I've experienced this with many businesses I've worked with, for example, in cafes and restaurants the latest refrigerators and freezers are much more energy efficient, much quieter and much more reliable. Same for ovens and dough mixers.

There are limits to this though, and it's not a competition to have better equipment than your competitors - in agricultural contracting businesses many owners seem to play the ego game of wanting to upgrade so they have the latest tractor, baler, digger, truck etc. Often the older one would have done a few more years and made the owner just as much money.

One way to minimize the attack on your profits is to consider leasing equipment and vehicles to allow your cash to be used for funding the business growth. Be careful though as a lease adds to your break even and hence your monthly cashflow.

PAYING CREDITORS EARLY

Sometimes I've found cashflow crunches exist because creditors have been paid too early, normally the thinking is 'Well, we had spare cash in the bank, so I thought I would get some creditors paid and out of the way'. Which sounds like a good idea but the danger here is not allowing for cashflow for the rest of the month, or, what about an unforeseen situation where a debtor can't pay you? I have also noticed a lot of business owners will pay all the smaller bills first to 'Get a bunch of them out of the way'. Then when it comes time to pay the larger bills (normally the suppliers) the piggy-bank is empty. Yes, sometimes it's a juggling act, but if your creditors terms are 20th of the month and it's only the first week, my advice would be to wait until due, you might as well have the money in your bank rather than someone else's.

LOAN OR MORTGAGE PAY DOWNS

Profit and cashflow crunches can be caused by loans that have been paid with lump sums over and above the normal payments. Like paying creditors, on the face of it this is a good thing, but not if it stresses the cashflow of the business.

THEFT OR SHRINKAGE

Theft could be happening in your business from customers or staff and you can track it in a few ways, regular stock takes and a constant review of your gross profit though your software is a good start. There's an old joke in the retail industry: 'If you are employing ten people in your business, then statistically one of them won't be stealing from you'! I like to think that people are much more honest than this, but the reality is that your profits and cashflow are affected hugely when any of your staff steal from you. Particularly if the theft is a product that has low margin, if an item has a margin of 10% gross profit, you need to sell another ten of them just to break even on the theft of the singular item! Cafes restaurants and bakeries are businesses that have many items that are tempting to staff such as cans of soda etc, but even the odd few hot fries or such like, start to add up if a few people are helping themselves over the course of a day.

Cameras can deter, but really the best course of action here is building a culturally honest atmosphere across the team and business, making sure to employ people with high ethics and developing an environment that they would never dream of stealing from you.

But, if you do have an instance where someone is clearly caught, either customer or staff, then make sure you follow appropriate procedures and take legal action. However - be consistent with your actions and consequences. Make it known that there is zero tolerance in your business for that kind of behaviour.

OWNERS DRAWINGS

The last place money can disappear in a business is one of the most obvious - the owners are taking too much money out for themselves. This can be because they have loans or mortgages to pay outside of the business, but it can also be to fund a certain level of lifestyle. Whenever I look though a profit and loss, I always want to know if 'wages' includes the owners (and maybe even pay-outs to their children), as well as looking at the drawings. Maybe the business cashflow is hemorrhaging because it just can't handle the amount of cash taken out. Sometimes it's as simple as increasing the profits or reducing the lifestyle.

As a side note, it goes without saying that taking cold hard cash out of a business causes shortfall and is 100% illegal as well. It also hampers a business owner from getting the best price for a business when they are ready to sell as there is no space in a sales and purchase agreement for 'Wink, wink, we take a lot of cash out'.

Some of My Streetwise Profit and Cashflow Strategies

Business Dashboard And The Grand Canyon Trip

I've been fortunate to have travelled extensively in America, starting in 1995 when I backpacked from New York on the east coast across to Seattle on the west coast in a horseshoe fashion via the southern states, so I've visited a lot of the outdoor natural attractions. It's an amazing country with a very diverse landscape. One of my favourite experiences was hiking into the Grand Canyon, what a massive achievement of quiet carving by the Colorado river over millions of years. Beautiful too. Every day many tourists choose to view the canyon by helicopters leaving from either Las Vegas or from the rim of the canyon, but I was too poor when I was backpacking and didn't take the chance when I was there last year either.

So, let's imagine a little scenario here. Imagine you are visiting the Canyon with your family, your wife and two teenage children. It's a beautiful day, the breeze is warm, the tourists are few and the views are so majestically stunning that even the children aren't actually staring at their phone screens for a change. You've watched a few of the tourist helicopters flying around, and in and out of the canyon and thought 'Wow that must be a nice way to get a different view'. Then you look over and you see a helicopter with a sign 'Canyon flight twenty minutes, only seventy-five dollars per person'. You nudge your wife and say, 'Hey we're not here every day, why don't we splash out and take a helicopter flight?' 'She says 'Yes let's do it, that would be wonderful'. You walk over and chat to the pilot, you all sign your names on a form, slip your credit card through the Visa machine and clamber into the seats of a Bell 206. It's all exciting and you focus on getting strapped in, headsets on, children all good. And then... you look down at the instrument panel and you see this:

The pilot then jumps in and proceeds to belt up, you tap him on the arm and say, 'Hey what's the story here, why are all these instruments taped up?' He says, 'Oh that, yeah, well I used to watch most of the instruments, but some stopped working and they were expensive to fix so rather than have them repaired I just taped over all the ones that I didn't really use, all I really need is the Attitude indicator as it tells me mostly what the helicopter is doing'.

Hmmm..., now it's decision time. Do you take the risk with your family and proceed with the flight, or do you bail out and ask for your money back?

I think most people would agree and take the bail out option, right?

The parallel here with business dashboards, is that the taped-up instruments in our Grand Canyon scenario helicopter, are pretty much how a lot of business owners run their businesses, they rely on one or two gauges (or indicators, or measurements), and ignore all the rest of the measurements they should be watching. They measure say, revenue for the month, expenses for the month, and did they make any money for the month. Which can work, for a while. However, this unsophisticated approach will more than likely cause the business to nose dive, maybe into a situation where it can't pull up again.

Running a business is pretty easy in good times if you have customers buying from you, your margins are ok, and you keep your expenses low, however it only takes a split second for things to change.

Here's an example of a few things that can change and are beyond your control:
- A new competitor comes into town (A lot more big chain stores are starting up, even in the smaller cities and towns).
- Government Policy changes (Changes to the Employment Act could mean the minimum wage has risen).
- Government Foreign Trade Policy (affects the rural backbone of a country with crops, meat, wool and dairy products prices, then trickles down to many other businesses that rely on agricultural dollars to grow and thrive).
- Health and Safety Regulations changes (this has been affecting trades businesses radically over the last few years).
- The weather and seasons (many businesses are affected directly by wind, rain, frosts or heat – sign writers, trades businesses, cafes, restaurants, architects etc.).

- Running expenses (fuel costs, freight and insurance have risen dramatically in the past few years).
- Universities and Polytechnics marketing direction for courses, (this has been affecting trades based businesses in New Zealand in recent years as there has not been as many young people pursuing an apprenticeship).

If you are running a business, the best contingency against a financial nosedive is to know the numbers in your business and track them like a grizzly bear on steroids. This way you can notice if something has changed and then do something about it. You can also make intelligent, informed decisions on what to invest money in, what products to promote, what expenses to reduce, when you can expand, or move to a bigger building and so on.

I need to point out at this stage that your money goal with your business isn't revenue, it's net profits. I learnt this a long time ago when a friend from Auckland and I were comparing businesses, he was talking about his wholesale fruit and vegetable business and said, "We had revenue of twenty million plus this year, it's been a great year" I said, "Wow that's amazing, time for a new Porsche?" He replied, "Well I only actually made about forty thousand and I'm not sure it was worth the stress".

Hmmm, I was thinking, isn't that interesting... one of my own businesses at the time had a revenue of $300,000 and I was making about $100,000 from it (without working in it myself). I know which business I would rather own!

Business owners worldwide generally have an ego about their business revenue and it's usually the artificial measure of success in a casual conversation. I always smile as I know the margins in a lot of industries and I know that large revenue doesn't necessarily equal large net profit for a business owner.

A small-scale mechanic business I worked with a few years ago is a great example of a potentially good business that was producing mediocre results because they weren't watching their numbers and making informed decisions. They contacted me saying they were tired of slogging it out, not making any money, and were thinking of closing it down to move on to something easier. First, I got them to find and print off a bunch of numbers for us to look at: Profit and loss for last three years, accounts receivables list in 30/60/90+ days format and chargeable hours each month split between hours charged and parts sold.

The first problem I could see was the turnover had been about the same for the past three years. Meaning that it could be they either had not acquired an increase of business from the year before and/or they had not raised prices for labour or parts.

	2015	2016	2017
Turnover/sales/revenue	$482,000	$460,000	$471,000
Gross Profit %	28.2%	29.0%	26.3%
Gross Profit	$135,924	$133,400	$123,873
Expenses	$96,000	$102,000	$115,000
Nett Profits	$39,924	$31,400	$8,873

Next problem; the Gross Profit was reducing 28.2%....29.0%....26.3%. Again, indicating that pricing wasn't matching at least, inflationary increases. More analysis revealed the expenses were climbing as well, and so the net profit was being eroded away. They were still working hard but had less to show for it. Is it any wonder they felt like giving up? Next up, we looked at the Accounts Receivable and did a quick calculation for the 'Debtor Days' (More about the importance of this number and how to calculate it on page 56).

Current	30 days	60 days	90 days	90 days +
	$41,000	$26,000	$11,000	$3,500

The debtor days calculated out like this: Total current debtors $81,500 divided by Annual Income (say $471,000 from last year) x 365 days = an average of 63.2 days to collect debt. The mechanics would complete work on a car and on average, not get paid until 63.2 days later (hint: BIG opportunity here to improve the cashflow).

On to chargeable hours, which the owners weren't sure about, so they had to go back and do some research. The resulting numbers looked like this for 2.5 mechanics (owner plus one fulltime mechanic plus one part-time fill-in guy): 2649 hours billed last year at $80 (inclusive of gst) = $211,950 of labour only.

Leaving $259,050 of revenue generated from sales of parts and consumables. Hours possible to be charged, approximate 2.5 people x 1808 (allowing for holidays, sick days and stats etc.) = 4520 hours possible. The ratio of hours charged vs. possible hours charged was: 4520hrs divided by 2649hrs = 58.6%.

> **NOTE:** The hours charged/billed vs. the possible hours that can be charged/billed ratio, is crucial for every business that is charging labour time at an hourly rate. For instance, a trades business or professional services type business.

So now that we knew some key numbers, what did we do? - I coached them to set up a business dashboard to track all these numbers accurately, most of them on a weekly basis. - We installed my accounts receivables system, and in fact, they outsourced the debt collection phone calls to a small company for the first few months with amazing results, getting in over $65,000 of the total receivables in about six weeks. Great for cashflow! - I coached them to increase their hourly rate from $80 to $88, more in line with what competitors were charging, after going through a mystery shopping process. This increased the profits of the business by $21,000 per annum.

- I helped the whole team improve their job card, time card and accuracy of information for each job, then coached the owners though making sure they were charging out what time each job was taking and not 'cranking back' the hours. This improved the charge out percentage to initially over 70%. Which equated to approx. 514 hours per annum or about 10 hours per week more being charged. This combined with the hourly rate increase created a huge gain of $66,512 per annum extra profit.
- We 'profit sliced' all expenses and made some savings of approx. $3,000 per annum.
- We price increased parts, on average, by 6% on approx. $270,050, giving extra profit of $16203 per annum (see chapter on increasing prices).
- I helped the owner carve out a set time each week to view, review , analyse and make decisions on the new dashboard numbers.

- Then we focused on what they would invest the new found profits in, rather than how they were going to pay their next bills ☺.

Cranking Back Hours:
Cranking back hours is a very common practice by either employees or the owner or both, it describes a process where the job took 7 hours, but the employee or owner looks at it, sucks though their teeth and thinks 'I can't charge that much, I'll reduce (crank) it back to 5 hours'.

It is often a misconception that the customer will protest about the bill or it can be caused from poor communication with a customer.

Occasionally it is a mistake made in the business and it may be legitimate to reduce the bill, but in most cases, better communication with the customer, for instance giving them a price range – 'If it all goes well the cambelt change will be around $600 but if we have trouble getting the pully off then it might be closer to $900', can reduce this happening to a minimum.

ACCURACY OF THE INFORMATION AND THE KITCHEN GUY

When it comes to measuring numbers, percentages and ratios in your business I can't over emphasize accuracy. I personally never trust numbers in my head for my businesses, and definitely don't trust numbers in my client's heads. I want to see the cold hard numbers sliced and diced in the accounting program or in a spreadsheet. Even then, we need to question each number and ensure it has been gathered and entered accurately.

Many years ago, I saw this first hand with a business coach that I knew fairly well and a kitchen manufacturing business he was working with.

The business was manufacturing kitchens in the lower dollar end of the market at around $10-$12,000 per kitchen and the coach asked the business owner 'How much profit do you make on these kitchens?' the owner said, 'Well the margins are tight but I'm positive we make about $750 profit on each one', 'Great' said the coach, 'Let's ramp up the marketing, increase your sales conversion and sell a heap more of these'.

All went well for a couple of months, more kitchens were sold, the conversion rate was spectacularly increased, and the business owner was extremely happy with how busy his business had become.

About three months later the coach got a call. 'We've had to pay the wages on the credit card for the past two weeks as we have no operating cash, we've looked at everything and can't see why we have a cashflow crunch'. [Whoop, whoop, whoop - sound of an alarm going off!] The business coach was very good at business improvement, had an accounting degree and was very experienced, however he had trusted numbers coming from someone's mouth, and not looked at the actual numbers in a spreadsheet. To cut a long story short, after a lot of analysis of revenue, expenses, debtors, creditors and cashflow, the coach and the business owner found, the true figures were actually a loss of $600 per kitchen! Thankfully they were able to save the business with some quick turnaround solutions, but, it's a big lesson for any business owner. You have been warned!

ACTION POINTS:

Set up a Business Dashboard specifically for your business. You probably already have the software and capability to do it, as most accounting programs have an abundance of features nowadays. Work hard on the accuracy of information in your business, good information in = good info out. Set up time for yourself to review the information you are measuring and make decisions on where you can next improve your business.

Here are a few dashboard ideas to get you started:

- Daily breakeven
- Weekly breakeven
- Weekly (or daily) revenue
- Gross profit
- Gross profit per product or service
- Debtor days (or accounts receivable days)
- Monthly breakeven
- Overall Net profit
- Stockturn ratio

Costs as a percentage of revenue (watch this carefully year on year).

For a service-based business, the hours you charge are key:
- Total hours charged out vs. possible hours to charge out
- Charge out hours per person per day, expressed as either hours or a percentage)

For a retail business:
- Number of customers and the amount they purchase is key
- Number of customers per day
- Average amount they spend in each transaction

- Overall gross profit margin
- Percentage margin on each product

For a business that quotes:
- Percentage of successful quotes and margin on those quotes are key:
- Number of quotes completed vs. number successful
- Gross profit margin on each quote as priced
- True gross profit margin of each successful quote (back costing is essential here)

For a manufacturing business:
- Efficiency of people and machinery, and the throughput of items produced is key.
- Number of widgets produced per day, per shift, per hour
- Number of widgets produced per person or per team

Managing/reducing expenses in your business, favored by most accountants, and to a certain point rightly so; minimizing expenses is important for two reasons:
1. To maximize profitability
2. To reduce the amount required to breakeven per week, month or year.

Anyone who runs a business knows that at some stage your cashflow is likely to dip below breakeven. It could be seasonal fluctuations, it could be when you're closed over the Christmas or Easter holidays or maybe when everyone leaves town for an event somewhere else, or it could be caused by a (normally temporary) surge of customers flocking from your business to the latest new cafe or shop in town.

Having a low breakeven really helps you get though these situations so looking at how to save unnecessary expenditure in your business is a good investment of time. However, you do need to keep it in perspective, as the diagram below shows, costs in your business can only be driven down so far whereas the top line of most businesses can be grown a lot.

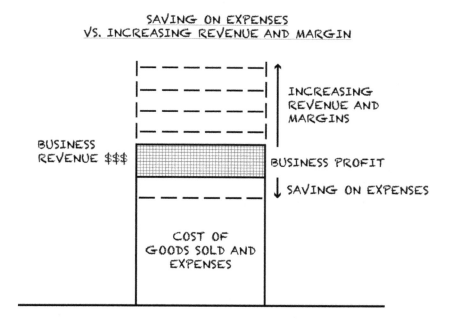

SAVING ON EXPENSES
VS. INCREASING REVENUE AND MARGIN

INCREASING REVENUE AND MARGINS

BUSINESS REVENUE $$$

BUSINESS PROFIT

SAVING ON EXPENSES

COST OF GOODS SOLD AND EXPENSES

In the first month of working with a new client I 'drive a bulldozer' though the P and L expenses to clean and clear things up and often find thousands of dollars in savings. Some of the places to look for savings are:

- Review of phone company deal
- Review of power company deal
- Review of fuel card supply deal
- Negotiating with all suppliers
- Review (and often slashing) advertising costs
- Setting goals around the wages bill, checking for overtime paid

NZ Waikato University Benchmark Statistics:
Each year many businesses throughout NZ contribute their year-end figures to the Waikato University where the information is collated into reports for industry types and business types.

Quite interesting to look through but be aware there can be some big differences with business size (overheads can get proportionally lower), and location (e.g. Auckland rent as a percentage of turnover is going to be a lot higher than Invercargill).

Ask your accountant if he can obtain a copy for your type of business but be sure to focus on the 'Top Three', not the 'Medium Performers'. You never want to be targeting your success on just average examples.

A friend said it nicely when I was racing motocross and watching the other classes for the best race lines. He said, 'Watch the top 3 guys, then turn your back, don't watch the bunnies, the lines they take ain't putting them on the podium'.

VEHICLES, PLANT, MACHINERY, AND OTHER SO-CALLED ASSETS.

Worth a chapter in its own, the purchase of cars, trucks, vans, office furniture and fittings, tools and machinery are often an over-spending area for a business owner. Much of the time it turns into ego purchases, which I like to call the 'flash factor', that is, most business owners want to have all the 'flashy' stuff.

Now, although these items fall under 'assets' in the balance sheet, most of them are actually 'liabilities' as they normally just cost the business money, not generate it. A business normally needs all these things to function but what this chapter is about is managing the expenses wisely.

Let's look at a typical trades business with a ute (pickup) or van. As you have probably noticed, most trades business owners have a new or nearly new ute, often something like a Ford Ranger or Toyota Hilux, both of which can cost well north of $60,000 especially when you start ticking options boxes.

The trouble is that the money needs to come out of the business in one way or another, either a cash payment, bank loan, lease deal or a lease to buy. A cash payment can hamper investment into other areas for growth, and wherever there is a monthly payment it raises the breakeven of the business. So, a lease payment of $800/month means the business needs to make another: $1,600/month at a GP of 50%, $2,000/month at a GP of 40%, $2,400/month at a GP of 30% and so on, and that payment is every month, even in those quiet months.

Now I do understand and take into account, that a business can't run on old clapped out vehicles, both from reliability, and from a business brand perspective. But often it's not a straight forward, black and white decision.

What are some options? Firstly, does your vehicle really need replaced, could it run another year or two? Or, do you just want the 'Flash Factor' so it looks like you are doing really well in business to your friends and family? The depreciation of a vehicle drops considerably in year two or three onwards. Just because the Ford dealer has offered you a nice new one with Apple Airplay at the same lease to buy per month doesn't necessarily mean you should jump - how long before you own the old one? What's it going to be worth if you wait another year (normally not much less).

Secondly, have you considered a low kilometer two or three-year-old, second-hand one? Often there are bargains out there when someone's situation changes. Or maybe an old model runout?

Personally, I've owned a lot of cars and SUV's (over eighty-five at last count, just don't tell my wife that number) and mostly European vehicles, which I love. But I've never brought one new. I wait to find one that has about 30,000ish kilometers on the clock and buy it for a third of what I would have to pay new. I've found if I enjoy them for a couple of years and sell with 70-80,000 kilometers, I lose very little money after all the gst and depreciation tax savings calculations.

You may think you need the new grill and headlights of the latest Ford Ranger or Audi, but I'll be honest with you, that one's going to look older as soon as the next one comes out anyway. You might not get the new car warranty with a less expensive second-hand car, but you will normally be able to buy a thorough breakdown warranty for less than $1000 per year (fully gst claimable and tax deductible)

Bank finance and leases, and also lease to buy deals can range hugely, but I seldom see a business owner look at every deal and then see if it can be negotiated. You're the customer here, and they want your business, so shop around. But, be wary of a low interest rate car dealer finance deal, there's probably a downside in there somewhere, and there are plenty of other independent finance companies to haggle with. Going independent also has the advantage you can buy any brand rather than jumping for a vehicle that has the lowest percentage rate advertised on TV. Be careful when adding all the extras too, nicer wheels, heated leather for your backside, Apple Airplay etc., somewhere, somehow, you'll be paying for all that bling.

QUIRKY SIDE NOTE: If you enjoy classic cars and trucks, then another option may be having one for your business, it will be slower, less comfortable, less economical, have few modern conveniences and maybe not be as reliable but it can be a point of difference that advertises your business when you drive around, and it won't date like a modern vehicle, or depreciate like a modern vehicle, in fact, it will probably go up in value.

I've seen this done successfully with 50/60/70's American pickups, Volkswagen Kombis and Beetles, old Fiat 500's, and even a Hillman Imp. One of my plumber clients is currently looking at an old Ford F-150 for the positive reasons above. It will likely be photographed a lot, so make sure your business name is highly visible on it somewhere. And, you have to be practical about it, I wouldn't advise this if you do a lot of kilometers, or drive up rough farm tracks etc., but it's food for thought.

OFFICE AND WAITING ROOM FITTINGS: Again, this is another area where business owners overspend with fancy desks, chairs, oil prints on the wall, and so on. Bear in mind, that most office furniture gets a hard life and will need to be replaced more quickly than your home furniture so, maybe it's better to buy a $350 Chinese version of that Barcelona chair rather than an original one at $4,500.

STOCKTURN IN A BUSINESS AND HOW TO MANAGE IT

In most businesses there is a certain level of stock (or inventory) required for the business to function, buying products in at wholesale, marking the price up and selling out at retail. There are huge advantages in minimizing the time and amount of stock you hold before selling it again, and this is why the 'Stockturn Ratio' or 'Rate of Stockturn' is so important to monitor.

It's also easy to calculate: Cost of Goods (COGs) sold per year/average stock in holding = Stockturn Ratio. COGs and the stock in holding number can easily be obtained from your annual P and L. Just make sure you do the calculation allowing for opening and closing stock. If you're not 100% sure how to do this, ask your accountant or email my team: admin@smallchangesbigresults.global

For example; a smallish supermarket client has a $3,100,000 per annum business with a COGs sold of $2,206,000 and a stock in holding of an average $119,000 at any time. $2,206,000/$119,000 = 18.54. This means he is turning over his stock 18.54 times each year, or about every 2.8 weeks. This number varies a lot between industry types and business stock mix, this particular supermarket sells a lot of fast food so the stockturn is higher than average.

Another example is a small cafe I am currently helping grow, their revenue is $260,000 per annum and stock in holding is only $6,000 so; $260,000/$6000 = 43.3 times per year or every 1.2 weeks

You can get the COGs number from your annual profit and loss and the stock in hand from your annual balance sheet as it's an asset to the business. You will have to take the opening and closing stock balances and add them together, then divide by 2 to get the average.

The aim here is to get your Stockturn Ratio per year as high as possible · which in effect means you are minimizing your stock holding and hence, the amount of money sitting around in the business. In some businesses it is possible to get this really high by effectively having a 'Just in Time' stock system, or even have raw goods or materials on consignment. I've helped a few trades based businesses like mechanics and engineers set this up.

QUIRKY CASE STUDY:

I was recently motorcycling with a couple of others in rural Cambodia and stopped at a little restaurant/shed/house on the side of a dirt highway. I had been told to not let appearances and the dirt floor get the better of me, this place made a fabulous hot noodle and meat lunch. We sat down and ordered (actually my Cambodian friend did all the ordering as not many rural people speak any English) and waited for our meal. I then noticed the chef mounting her scooter and tearing off down the road, returning a few minutes later with some meat. She preceded to prepare it quickly and start it cooking, then tore off down the road again, this time in the opposite direction and returning with the vegetables.

My thought - what an ultimate stock system for a restaurant, a 'just in time' system where there were only minutes between buying the raw goods and getting paid for the cooked meal!

Another way of improving your stock turn and minimizing having your own dollar notes tied up in stock on the shelf, is to negotiate a consignment deal with a supplier. This is where a supplier allows you to have a stock level of their product in your business, as long as it is being used, and you pay for it as soon as it's used. They are usually willing to do this as it cements you as a customer because you now have all their product in your store. It works well as long as there is trust between the two parties and the supplier systems are accurate.

I was involved with setting up consignment stocks at the NZ dairy giant Fonterra's milk processing plants, and learnt it is fantastic for smaller businesses as well. Normally a sales rep will come in and restock each week or two and this saves you the time and energy of putting an order in. I've done this with engineering and electrical businesses in the past and it's particularly good if the stock is really expensive, for instance, hydraulic hoses and fittings. And also, good if your business has a 24/7 breakdown promise and service. Rather than you carrying $30,000 of product to cover any contingency, your supplier fronts the cost and restocks it as you use and sell it.

DEBTOR DAYS RATIO AND HOW IT AFFECTS YOUR BUSINESS

The debtor days ratio shows how good your systems are at getting the money in that is owed to you in the timeframe you have allowed. This length of time is traditionally monthly in New Zealand, but (thankfully), more and more businesses are changing to seven-day invoicing, meaning they expect to be paid within seven days of the invoice generation date. The ratio is calculated by simply dividing the debtors by the invoiced sales (in some businesses this won't be the total revenue of the business, due to a combination of instantaneous cash or card sales).

Taking one of my mechanic clients as an example: $451,000 overall annual revenue but $213,000 invoiced over the year (so $238,000 is cash or card sales) Debtors $22,000. So: 22,000/$213,000 x 365 days = 37.7 days on average to collect the debt owed.

Is this a good or bad number? Well it depends on the terms of trade, in this situation we are on thirty-day invoicing and moving towards seven-day invoicing so it's not bad but can, (and will) get better. Note - sometimes in a business like this you may be waiting on a sub-contractor's bill, e.g. an auto electrician to come in, and so it can be difficult to get the invoices out quickly. But I've always found this will be an exception rather than the norm, so, the goal is to get 95% of the invoices generated as fast as possible and then followed up if there is a delay in payment. The more effectively you can manage the debtor days, the better the cashflow will be in the business and it is a key ratio to be constantly monitoring.

CASH GAP AND THE BATHROOM FITTINGS GUY

Many of the areas that money disappears in a business are to do with timing of the money in and out of the business – this concept is technically called 'Cash gap'.

Cash Gap is caused by a difference in timing, between when a company buys stock or materials, and when payment is actually received from the customers, and can commonly stretch out to ninety days or more for a business if it is not watched and monitored carefully. Just like boarding the underground tube train at Piccadilly Circus, you need to 'Mind the Gap', the Cash gap.

The CASH GAP Dilemma

CASE STUDY:

A bathroom fittings importer and retailer I worked with for a few years had a cash gap that was causing him stress and putting the business in a position where it couldn't afford to pay bills on time each month, worse still, the owner desperately wanted to expand and couldn't get finance to buy more product from overseas because he was always maxing out his overdraft.

The situation looked like this, using an example of fittings at cost of $6,000 and retail of $10,000; he would get a set of plans for a house, price it up for fittings, have the quote approved by vendors, then order the fittings from overseas and pay for them at thirty days. The fittings took three months to get to NZ, sometimes another month before they were unpacked in his store. No deposit or progress payments were invoiced or taken, and he didn't get paid until they were installed, usually thirty days after they were installed. His cash gap looked like this:

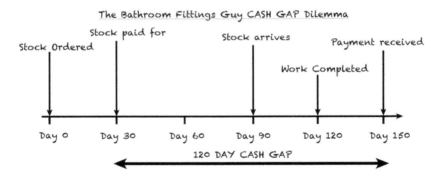

You can see how his cashflow was minimized and he was in effect, acting as a bank for his suppliers and also his clients. In order to grow and expand his business we needed to make some changes! So how did we fix this?

First, we phoned the overseas suppliers and negotiated a payment schedule of paying only 20% for the goods within thirty days once the shipping order was processed, then another 20% when they cleared NZ customs, and the final payment thirty days after they arrived at his store. They were ok with doing this as **a)**. He's a $700,000 customer and they didn't want him to change suppliers. **b)**. He had been trading with them for years, never a hassle and always paid on time. Bear in mind, each container of fittings he was shipping had a value of over $100,000.

Then we had a solicitor write up a new sales contract to get 100% refundable deposits from customers once the quote was confirmed, first 33% (but later I actually encouraged him to take it to 60%). Then another 33% when the fittings cleared customs and the balance of full payment within seven days once the fittings were on site.

I coached him on how to position the client about the 33% deposit, the 33% progress payment and the payment expected within seven days once the fittings were on site. Using the same example of fittings at cost of $6,000 and retail of $10,000 the cash gap now looked like this:

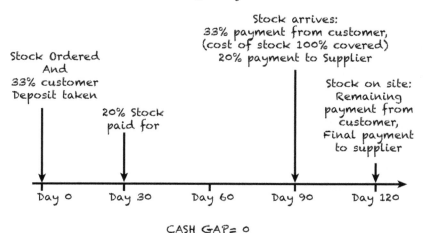

The Bathroom Fittings Guy CASH GAP Fix

You can see that now he was actually getting paid for all cost of the fittings before he had to pay the suppliers fully, and he reduced his overdraft to zero. We went on to double the physical size of the business (and moved to a larger site), and double the revenue, but couldn't have done so without reducing the cash gap.

Now you may think this is hard to believe but the reality is, how often do people buy bathroom fittings for their dream home? Once or twice in their lifetime? With carefully worded positioning after they had confirmed the quote, how would anyone know or think the process of payments was any different?

I have installed a similar process in many other business types – just because the industry has done it a certain way for years, doesn't mean you can't make your own rules, as long as you 100% deliver on your side of the commitment.

Calculating your own business's cash gap is easy: Add the average days in stock, to the average collection period for accounts receivable, and subtract the average payment period for accounts payable.

Remember that the cashflow is the lifeblood of a business so make sure you are monitoring all of the seven areas mentioned, and if you haven't got a Cashflow forecast in place (cash based not accrual), then you may not see a cashflow crisis coming and be able to prepare for it.

PRICING TO MAKE DECENT PROFITS

Pricing in any business is important, in fact it's about as important to business survival as having at least 20% oxygen in the air you breathe every day.

Most business owners are frightened to increase their pricing as they think they will drive customers away. Now I agree there are some staple items in businesses that are price sensitive, but there will be many others that are not so delicate. I owned a supermarket that had a GP % of 15.4% when I brought it but within six months I had raised it to 28.6%, mostly though smart pricing.

Think about that for a moment – the profitability has almost doubled without an increase in Cost of Goods sold, without any fancy advertising, and, without losing customers.

So how could that work? Well the first thing to realize is that the same product sold in different ways can have a variety of different prices. As a quick example, did you ever whip down to the gas station or corner store to buy some milk when you knew that you could definitely buy it cheaper at the supermarket? Same milk, probably in the same packaging. Or have you ever brought an ice cream or popcorn at the movies, knowing you were paying twice as much as you would at the store just around the corner?

If you feel like bringing Chinese takeaways home for dinner after a long hard day at work, you probably know you could have brought the ingredients for around ten dollars from the supermarket rather than pay twenty dollars from the takeaway shop. And if you decided it would be much nicer to sit in a quiet restaurant atmosphere and have Chinese food served to you, then you are probably eating the same cost of ingredients but paying forty-five dollars. Same ingredients, different experiences.

So, price may not be the only factor, but here's one more example to drive this home: You are planning on remodeling the bathroom in your home and it's going to cause some disruption. There are going to be builders, electricians, plumbers, tilers and painters traipsing through your home and, to top it off you only have one shower, so minimum downtime is essential, so you don't out-live your welcome showering at the in-law's place.

Now here's the question: Would you rather engage a builder who is the cheapest but has a reputation for being slow and disorganized, or would you rather pay more and have a builder who is superb at project managing his team and also the subbies. His reputation for quality is also unprecedented, ensuring everything is done right the first time and no-one needs to come back and fix anything. It's a no-brainer, right?

Many business owners ask me the question: 'How much should I be charging?' (I was asked this again last week by a local engineer), or, 'What margin should I be charging, or mark-up should I put on?' There are a few ways to price products and services in your business.

- Price according to your marketplace, (local, national or even global)
- Recommended retail pricing- Cost Plus Pricing - expenses plus profit pricing
- Mark-up pricing (usually expressed as a percentage)
- Marketplace price testing

Some businesses use a combination of several of the above methods. I could ramble on here about all kinds of ways to do this, but let me illustrate something with a story:

I was speaking in Memphis, Tennessee a few years ago, to a group of business coaches, mostly from America. I think there were about two-hundred people in the room, and I was speaking about ways to increase pricing in a business. I was using a service-based business with an hourly rate as an example and I asked the question: 'If we want to increase the hourly chargeable (called billable in the USA) rate in this business, how would we determine how much to increase it?' Several hands shot up and each person proceeded to explain to the audience some complicated way of working it out usually with 'National Medium Hourly Rate' in there somewhere. One guy actually wanted to obtain a standard deviation bell curve graph and then apply a calculation to it. After a few of these answers I said 'Whoa, whoa, whoa, how about this.

How about we just do a quick mystery shop of the 3-5 competitors and then raise it five dollars per hour?' Holding my hand in the air with 5 fingers spread out to emphasis my point. The audience went silent (Apart from the sound of some lightbulbs inside of heads going on).

The point of me telling you this story, is that I think most business owners overcomplicate how to price. I can do complicated, in fact I like complicated (I was a marine engineer originally remember?) But, pricing doesn't need to be complicated, so let's be practical about it.

It usually doesn't really matter what the national average is for your product or service if your customers are local. It doesn't matter what the global average is for your product or service if you are selling nationally. (There is a caveat here if you are selling something that can be brought off the internet and shipped easily and cheaply to an end user). Your aim is to be the highest priced in the market, and then provide the most amazing service or experience for the customer or client.

> And in a trades business you can always use the cliché of:
> 'Well you can have any 2 of these: Low price/fast speed/amazing quality - but not all 3 of them'.

No matter what business you are in there will be some part of it where you can increase pricing in some way. And, as I mentioned earlier, some items can be price sensitive, in my supermarket, milk, bread, newspapers, cheese, coke cola and many other items had to be at a certain price. Did I care? Nope, there were seven-thousand lines in my store, so plenty of scope to increase the GP. Price according to your marketplace, local, national or even global. In the coaching franchise I own we have a strategy for increasing profits that says, 'Increase all prices by 10%', but I've always thought that it was a little too crude as there is usually more scope with many items.

A good place to start is to run a stock report by 'numbers of items sold' and start with the highest volume products first. Reason being, if you are selling an item once per month and you raise the price by fifty dollars, then you've made enough extra each month to eat out for lunch once. But, if you increase the price on a high-volume item that you are selling hundreds or even thousands of each month, then a small pricing difference can give you a BIG result.

I proved this many years ago with one of my first business coaching clients when we raised the price of his guitar picks from 50 cents to $1.20 (we checked local pricing first), we tracked it consistently and the sales remained the same at around 4000 picks per year. That little plastic triangle shaped pick then generated: 4000 x 70cents increase = $2800 per annum extra profit, no extra cost of goods, no fancy marketing. Then we moved onto the next line which was guitar strings, then sheet music then …

COST PLUS PRICING

If you are already doing cost plus pricing, then it might be time to review against the market and increase the percentage you are adding on. One thing I do like about this method, is that the price continues to move when there is an increase in the raw cost of goods. If the product comes into the business at say $100 and is marked-up by 30% to $130.00, then next month if the product comes in at $102 then the price will automatically rise to $132.60.

MARKETPLACE PRICE TESTING

This strategy is a little bolder but can be very effective. Basically, you keep increasing your prices up and up until you sense some market resistance. And I don't mean a giant survey of one or two people, I mean when the product sales start noticeably dropping, then you are probably at the upper end of what the market will accept. One of my service station clients used to do this with hot pies and he could tell by the weekly figures if he had reached the upper limit or not.

CASE STUDY:

I worked with a lovely couple who owned a very specialized glass business, they had the perfect combination of one person being very arty and creative and the other partner being very practical and logical, and they were producing an amazing product, in fact, I would say it was world class.

When discussing their product lines and how well they were selling we talked about a beautiful handmade one-off, no-two-the-same glass platter they made and sold. They told me they weren't selling as many of these as they would like and had quite a stockpile as they would always make one if they had a spare space in the furnace alongside a larger shower door or similar.

I asked them the price and they said they sold it for $60. "Whoa' I said, 'you're kidding right?" "No, why?" I replied, "Well it looks to me like it's a piece of art but you're selling it at a price similar to what I would have to pay for a mass produced one at a local store. How about we raise the price?"

Long story short after much discussion and a little market research we raised the price to $150 and repositioned how they were sold using words like:
Totally unique
One-off
No two the same
Handmade
Designed locally

- Result - sales of the platter doubled.

Most times the resistance to a higher price is in your head, not the customers.

> ***Final note:*** Please don't be afraid of raising your prices in your business, you are in business to make a profit and if you don't make enough profit, you won't be able to stay in business to service your customers' needs and wants for years to come.

ACTION POINTS:

> - Analyse the pricing in your business with a fine-toothed comb, it is the lifeblood of your business and you are better to be constantly edging the prices up than realizing in two years' time after no pricing increases, you now need to make a big jump up to where you need to be in the marketplace.
> - Only look at your main competitors, don't worry about pricing compared to others that your customers wouldn't go to anyway.
> - Start with the highest volume items in your business and analyse weather you can shift the pricing a little, or a lot. - Back up your higher pricing with outstanding service and an amazing experience for the customer.

MYSTERY SHOP AND IMPROVE THE SELLING PROCESS.

Sales and the sales process in most businesses are a very under maximized area. Many books have been written on the subject of selling but I have found very little explaining in detail about how to improve the sales process in totality. So, let's focus on applying some small changes to give big results to the process.

When a lead (prospect) connects with your business though email, phone or face to face, there is a reason they came to you. And aside from A-grade referrals, almost every lead has cost the business in some way. This is called acquisition cost and can vary wildly from very expensive (TV, radio, print media) to inexpensive (business cards, branded pens, networking).

Acquisition cost per strategy also varies with time for a particular marketing medium, an advert in a local rural newspaper could be visible to your audience for just a few days, whereas signage on a building could generate leads for years. It's beyond the scope of the sales process topic here but calculation of acquisition cost from any, and all monies spent/invested in marketing activities is crucial when making future marketing decisions.

My main point here is that if it costs to get someone to contact you about your products or services, wouldn't it make sense to do all that you can to make sure they purchase from you? And, continue to purchase many times after that? And, refer their friends and family to purchase from you as well?

When I say, 'Do all you can', I mean everything that makes the buying process enjoyable, (even fun maybe), efficient and totally 100% tailored to their needs and requirements. To the point where they would say, 'Why would I bother going anywhere else?'

It's also good at this stage to know what you are up against in the marketplace, who are your competitors? If the prospect doesn't buy from you then who would they buy from? And what is their sales process like? It's not essential to know this but it's always interesting and usually quite surprising. And by the way, you don't have a hundred competitors. Most business have three to five main competitors and you will know who they are.

Mystery shopping a competitor's sales process is an exercise I often coach my clients through and we track many aspects to give an idea of how and what we can do to improve the prospect experience with us.

Let's look at the tabulated findings from a flooring company I did this with recently. See the image on the next page.

	Response after initial enquiry	Time for initial enquiry	Quote delivered Email or in person	Follow up on quote	Follow up on quote again
Client's company	Same day	1 Day	Both	1 Week	Within month
Competitor 1	2 Day	3 Day	Email	None	None
Competitor 2	Same day	Still waiting			
Competitor 3	Same day	1 Week	Email	None	None
Competitor 4	3 Day	8 Day	Email and Ph. call	1 Week	None

As shocking as these results appear, I've come to realize over the years that results like this are very common and always exciting for my clients as it indicates there is huge scope to be best in the marketplace. (Which means prices can be the highest as well).

The problem is, nobody seems to map out the sales process in any detail, and then tweak and refine it to make something amazing. A common business sales process for a business that quotes work, from initial enquiry to dollars in the bank for the business might look like this:

OLD SALES SYSTEM

INITIAL ENQUIRY — SITE MEASURE — DELIVER QUOTE BY EMAIL — PH. CALL FOLLOW UP — BOOK DATE AND COMMUNICATE — COMPLETE JOB — $$$ IN BANK

Which on the face of it looks ok, however, if we really wanted to stand out we could make the experience something special if the process looked more like this:

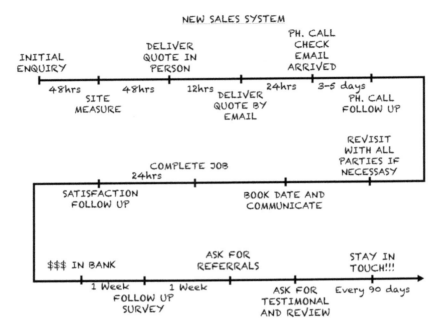

As you can see, there are much more contact points or 'touches' in the second process to take the prospect on the journey to becoming a buying customer, and various ways of implementing the touches as well, such as phone, email and text. These touches build rapport and also allow the business to really hone in on what the customer really wants and needs.

There are also timing Key Performance Indicators (KPI's) to ensure, a). The sales step happens in a timely fashion and b). The steps aren't happening too quickly and overbearing the prospect or annoying them. Note: these steps and timings need to be customized for every business and will differ for different product types, different target markets and different industries.

In our floor covering business example above we have slightly different process steps depending on the dollar value of the work, and also a different process if it is residential, industrial or commercial work.

Don't get hung up on the number of steps, frequency, timing etc. on the diagram on the previous page, just take the concept and apply it to a review of your current system.

And if you really want to maximize the relationship you now have with the customer, then there is a lot you can include in your aftersales as well. If you're giving the customer a wonderful buying experience wouldn't it make sense to ask them for feedback, ask them for a testimonial, ask them for referrals, ask them to do a Facebook or TripAdvisor review; keep in touch with them so they buy from you again?

Most businesses throw away the opportunity for any of the above because they are too focused on moving onto the next customer.

ACTION POINTS:

Map out your current sales process with timings for each step implemented.

Be honest with yourself and mark yourself 1-10 on each step, with 1 being a Dull experience to 10 being a mind-blowingly 'Wow'! experience for the customer.

Break it down, improve every piece and re-assemble...

INCREASING AVERAGE SALE SIZE

One of the easiest, and best ways to increase your business's revenue and profitability is to sell more products and services to your existing clients. Up-selling and Cross-selling, increasing the average sale size by a little (or a lot).

Good upselling is an art. It's all about timing and relevance to the customer enjoying themselves or benefiting from the upsell. How many times have you been at a restaurant, finished your meal and the waiter asks, 'Now, would you like to see the desert menu?' and if you say, 'No thanks', then he politely asks, 'How about coffees then, or perhaps a little nightcap?'

That's upselling selling right there and it is in no way about manipulating customers. The most effective way to sell more to someone is when they have a genuine interest in it anyway. The textbook example is the McDonald's 'Would you like fries with that?'. That one small question allows McDonalds to sell over four-million extra kilograms of fries globally every day. And, they don't stop there. McDonalds' employees then ask every customer if they would like a drink or larger sizes. The statistic that is banded around is that three out of ten people will buy on an up-sale. I remember going through a McDonalds drive-through after a day's motorcycle racing, a bunch of us in a car with motorcycles on the trailer, and when the girls voice came out of the order box 'thing' and began upselling, everyone in the car was saying 'yes', 'yes', 'yes', except me. 'Up-size your drink for only a dollar?' 'Yep', 'Upsize your fries for only a dollar more?' 'Yep'. I thought, 'Wow, that was really interesting, that upsell phrasing really works!'

The incremental increases to the average dollar spend due to these small cross and up sells, do wonders to boost any business's bottom line and McDonalds knows this from experience with sixty-nine million customers per day being asked to buy more.

Now before you think: Hey I don't want to blatantly upsell like a fast food chain! I am not here to suggest you take the same approach with your professional clients. But, what I am highlighting is that cross-selling and up-selling is an established and well recognized sales technique, that most people accept as normal and actually expect. So why not investigate how it could help your business?

We all know it costs a lot less to keep a client, than to find another one. And it costs a whole lot less to sell more to an existing client than it does to find new clients. Selling more to these clients is quite different to selling to new clients too. They already understand your reputation, your skills and the quality of your advice and service. They already know you, probably like you, know how it works, and probably want to deal with you again. Of these things your client is already convinced.

The key is to demonstrate an understanding of their needs, and then bring to their attention useful products or services that you can also provide. As long as you are suggesting products or services that are appropriate, they will most probably genuinely appreciate the offer. And by the way, the last thing you want to hear from any of your customers is 'Oh I didn't know you sold that/did that, I just brought one of those from [insert your arch rival competitor here]'

Of the many clients you have interacted with recently, how many only really know about the products that they have bought from you? Do they know what other services you provide? Don't assume they do. When people buy something, they are usually focused only on that one thing, and simply telling your clients about all your products and services can bring in more business on its own.

Imagine a café waitress who chats away to you and casually mentions, 'Oh we also make whole cakes to take away too'. Or a plumber who says, 'Oh we have a little hire truck too if you're looking to put some gravel on your driveway' Or a doctor who says, 'Oh I do amputations as well if you're looking to remove a limb'. Maybe not the doctor one, but you get my message.

Here's some ideas to get you thinking about how to sell more and increase your average sale size:
- Brainstorm a list of products or services that match up with what a customer is already buying from you
-Invest in development of yourself and your team in the process and skills of cross-selling
-Introduce a wider range of contact points to a client (as detailed in systemizing your sales process)
- Change your marketing approach to added value

ACTION POINTS:

- Upselling to increase the size of the sale is normal and mostly expected

- Your clients like you and are probably keen to buy other things from you

- Brainstorm a list of products and services that to match what is being purchased

- Your team and probably yourself probably need some training on how to subtly upsell in your business – get in touch with me if you need help with this.

THE POWER OF SYSTEMS IN A BUSINESS AND MY OWN SUPERMARKET OPERATIONAL MANUAL

I first learnt the power of systems with my early childhood business, then later with a bulk delivery distribution business and also my supermarket. I was kind of forced to create systems for most of my businesses as I was mostly working a full-time job as well in the early days of being a business owner.

I'm a big fan of an operational manual in a business and here's the simple story that convinced me. In my supermarket business, we had a lot of waste cardboard boxes as everything would arrive in boxes and need unpacked to be put out on the shelves, and as you can imagine with a couple of trucks of product turning up each week we had enough boxes to package Christmas presents for a hundred years. We gave away a lot to people who were shifting house etc., but we still had a cardboard box trash problem. Our recycling skip out the back was on a monthly hire plus a charge to empty it regardless of weight, so just based on volume. When it was full, it got emptied and they would send me a bill. I instructed everyone who worked for me that we needed to fold and cut the boxes to flat-stack them in the skip, thereby maximizing the volume of cardboard we could get taken away for a single bill. This went along fine until one day I flicked the lid up and it was full of complete boxes rather than flat-stacked. I remembered that we had just employed a new team member and a lightbulb went on – we need a system so this never happens again. This was the trigger that started me writing an Operations Manual for the business. Starting with instructions on how to pack the recycling skip!

Having a comprehensive operations manual meant there were very few incidents like this in the future, but it also meant that the cost of training someone became much less. When we employed someone, we would print a copy of the operations manual with their name on the front and give it to them when they came in to sign the employment agreement.

99% of people would take this away and read through so when they started a few days later, they were already familiar with how a lot of processes worked. And if they asked a question about something we would always say 'Have you checked the manual?' If they had and it still wasn't clear, we would amend the description or instructions for that process or task. If the questions were about something that wasn't currently in the manual then, guess what? We would add another section into the contents.

Don't take this example as too simplistic, the result of this decision to systemize absolutely everything I could in every business I owned, was a game changer, saving much time and money for myself and also for my team.

I've written in other chapters about the power of having a comprehensive sales system, systems for tracking your business dashboard, an accounts receivable system, systems for increasing profits, stock control systems etc., but how do you actually start writing systems for your business? The place I start is getting an owner to list all the tasks that he/she is doing daily/weekly/monthly etc., then at the same time, get each team member to do the same. This basically creates a draft set of contents for your operational manual. When setting up systems in your business, make sure you also include:

Marketing:
You should have systems to measure where all your leads are coming from. It can be as simple as asking 'So whereabouts did you hear about us?' I remember when Yellow Pages started to go online, and I was working with a large electrical business, they were investing (spending) over $25,000 per year in paper book Yellow Pages ads. We had been talking about it and were going to cut it right back to approximately $10,000, then the results of asking new clients started coming in. You guessed it, there were a ton of leads coming from the Yellow Pages!

Split testing of ads is a great system to narrow down which ad, which offer, which picture and so on, gives you the best lead generation. Nowadays, this is relatively easy if you are marketing on any form of social media.

Selling
Systems to train your team how to greet and treat customers, how to quietly upsell, how to close a deal, how to sell a higher margin product. These type of training systems are not just for sales teams, everyone in your business is a face to the business, weather you are selling coffees in a café or life insurance to corporate executives.

Customer-service
In my mind, this is something that New Zealand businesses could learn more from businesses overseas, particularly America which generally has outstanding customer service (maybe that's a good reason for a tax-deductible research trip to the USA).

What you are aiming to achieve here is a consistently out-standing experience for the customer from every single person involved in your business. From the lady who polished or vacuums the floor to the accounts receivable person (who hasn't struck a grumpy one of those?), to the front-line people dealing with the customers or clients. Even the way everyone answers the phone should be systemized.

Systems don't just have to be in written form, they can be developed as training videos, photos of 'how to' or training programs on a computer. One system I have personally used to create a system in my coaching business is to video my Mac screen while I voice over, then send it to my PA. It saves me writing everything or typing everything out and it means she has the video on file to reference back to anytime.

The easiest way I've found of documenting how a certain task is done, is to get the person who is already frequently doing that task to write or record how they do it. Even better if you can get the input of a few of the team who are doing the same task, as between them, it will be easy to find the 'best practice' that gets the task done to the highest degree in the shortest time.

You can also have different manuals for different roles, like a manual for a manager vs. a manual for a waiter and different manuals for different parts of your business. A kitchen operation manual (I need one of those for myself at home!), a marketing manual, a selling and customer service manual.

There are also future benefits to having great systems in your business should you decide to license it, franchise it or even grow your business though acquisition of a competitor or a branch in another area/province/town/city.

Systems will also add value to your business when it comes time to sell, as buyers are usually looking for 3 main things: Does it make good money? Is there potential to grow it some more? How much of my time will it take to run it?

ACTION POINTS:

- Any time invested in building systems now will save you time in the future.

- Don't be overwhelmed with the idea of setting up systems in your business, start small with a table of contents.

- Systems don't have to be in a written format, it's ok to have a photo showing how the workplace should look when a job is finished, or a training video with ideas of what to say to people for great customer service.

- Get the team involved in writing the systems.

- Remember to look at EVERYTHING, not just the obvious, think to yourself 'What else would McDonalds systemize here?'

- Systems will save you time and money when it comes time to replace a team member

Invest time building systems now, so you save more time for yourself later.

[6[

MARKETING FOR
THE BEST TEAM MEMBERS

Have you ever found yourself saying or thinking, 'It's just so hard to get good people nowadays'? That could be because employment and recruiting has changed. Long gone are the times when you could run an advert in a local paper saying;

'MECHANIC WANTED', or 'OFFICE MANAGER WANTED'.

Even though there are probably about the same amount of jobs available and about the same amount of people looking for a job (varies per sector of course), nowadays it's not about advertising, it's about marketing.

What I mean is, if you want to have the best people, you have to do the best marketing to attract them to enquire with you. Sounds wrong doesn't it? You having to do the work to attract people, after all it's you that's taking the risk on employing them, and it's you, providing them with an opportunity to earn money. Sorry but this is old school thinking and I've seen many business owners get hung up on this. The truth is, the methods of recruiting great people have changed.

It all starts with the job advert, and the question I always ask when reviewing an employment ad is: 'Why would an amazing person come and work for you based on this ad?' And that one question unlocks one of the secrets to finding the best people!

Years ago, when I had an interest in my brothers' silage harvesting business, I suggested we should change the way we were writing the ads and also the process an applicant went though. We wanted reliable people who were great operators, but also diligent and careful with the machinery and could work with the team and with the clients. Most of the competing silage harvesting guys wanted the same people of course, so I figured we needed to out-market them. We started by listing all the benefits of working for our silage business, and also incorporated some of the core values we were looking for into the ad. We also listed the benefits of working in this area of New Zealand, as in the past we had frequently had replies from overseas as well.

The results were solid, we started to attract a better type of applicant, more aligned to our company values. We then developed an application questionnaire, a nice cover letter and included the full list of ten core values that we expected the team work to.

Another solid result and many applicants did fill in the questionnaire and get it back to us, those that didn't, we didn't bother going any further with – we figured if they weren't going to take the time to fill it in, then they weren't serious enough about the job for us. Overall result was a much better-quality applicant and of course much better employees, aligned with how the company ran.

The ad you write needs to firstly attract someone to read or click further, so like all other marketing, the headline is key: 'Passionate Chef with flair wanted' will probably get more interest than 'Chef wanted'. 'Engineer looking for great pay, 8-5 hours and interesting work', will probably get more interest than 'Engineer Wanted'. Don't worry if you think your headline is too long – it isn't if it attracts attention.

Try to centre your headline on the benefits for the person. In the engineer example, I know there are multitudes of job opportunities for engineers, but a lot of them require long hours or shift work, some of the jobs are uninteresting as well, doing repeat engineering work day in and day out. If you are looking to attract a guy who is settled with a couple of children, 8-5 hours might really suit him. Conversely, shift work or long hours may appeal to a younger person looking to build up their bank balance quickly. It is worth brainstorming some headlines with your team, partner or a business coach.

The body of the ad also needs to focus on WIIFMe (What's In It for Me), so what are the benefits for the candidate? And you need to be clear what the job is and what it isn't, otherwise you'll get a lot of people coming in the top of the funnel that could waste your time. For instance, you may want to put, 'Must be qualified welder', and, 'Must have full License'. These phrases will narrow the funnel down.

Lastly, you need a *Call to Action* – tell them what to do next. I like things that are a little different, mainly to see if they will follow instructions. Apply by emailing xxxxxxxx@xxxx.com for an application pack, be sure to include your resume with references. Rather than 'Phone xxxxxxxxxx'

Over the years I've helped many businesses set up their question and application pack and it differs from business to business, but one thing we always ask for is for it to be hand written. This means we can also check handwriting and grammar (useful in more businesses than you would expect), although I suspect many male applicants get their wife or partner to fill it in!

At the same time, we are setting the ad and recruitment process up, we also have to decide where to place the ad or ads. This is under-looked by most business owners and is a similar process to working out where your target market is located for selling your products and services.

I have actually built a simple recruitment course that will transform your recruitment process. Contact me if you'd like to know more...

THE APPLICANT FUNNEL AND THE FUNNY PACIFIC ISLAND RESULT

I believe any type of marketing is like a funnel, and there is a certain number of people you want to enter the top of the funnel; not too many, not too few, just the right number, kind of like Goldilocks' porridge.

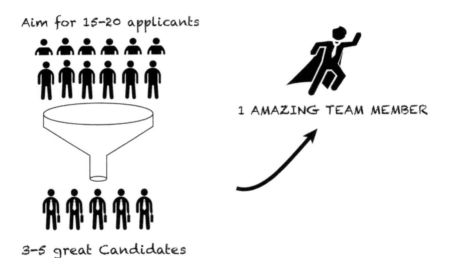

APPLICANT FUNNEL

Aim for 15-20 applicants

1 AMAZING TEAM MEMBER

3-5 great Candidates

Funnel size is important: A few years ago, I helped a forestry business owner recruit for workers on a certain pacific island. He wanted sixteen good keen strong guys to work hard in the forestry for good pay. We cast the net wide and advertised in a few places with his email as the contact method. A few days after the ads had been placed he called me and said: "Hey Andrew, we've got a problem with those ads". Surprised, I said "What, have you had no replies?" He said "No, the opposite, I have over 4,000 replies in my inbox". Pause. "Whoa, tell you what, press ctrl A and then delete, we need to start again". I figured there was no way he would be able to deal with over 4,000 emails.

Funnel too wide, let's start again! ...

The second time around we only advertised though the island churches and had a much more manageable number, resulting in sixteen fantastic employees.

A prime reason to have only a few people apply is that you don't want to end up interviewing a bad bunch and then choosing the best of that bunch. My rule of thumb is twenty people apply in the top of the funnel, then narrowed down to three to five for interviews, this will normally give a good result. Generally, the more people that apply, the more choices you'll have to narrow it down to the last three to five for interviews. And for heaven's sake, if you don't get the right person in the first round, make sure you analyse the marketing and market the position again.

Sometimes we outsource the handling of the applicants, the emails back and forth etc., especially if the business owner is very busy. (He/she is probably busy because that role hasn't been filled yet). If the person you outsource to for this stage is well informed on what you are looking for, they will easily narrow the applicants down for you.

PLACES TO ADVERTISE FOR TEAM MEMBERS

Here are some of the places I've successfully marketed for people. Keep an open mind when you read this list as some of these you may dismiss too quickly. They could be worth a try for your business too.
- On your email signature
- On the bottom of your invoices
- Temporary Building signage

- On the back window of trades vans
- On Facebook – get your friends to share as well
- In school newsletters
- In church newsletters
- Asking your suppliers
- Asking your customers
- Asking your best team members, (like attracts like)

The most interesting thing I think I've found about recruitment with businesses is that most business owners invest very little time into development of an amazing recruitment system and yet they are prepared to make a huge investment of their money into people who work in their business. If you employ someone at say $40,000 per year and they stay with you for 3 years, you've invested $120,000 into that person and position in your business. Wages in most businesses are one of the major expenses. Wouldn't it make sense to do everything you can to get the recruitment right? And don't get me started on what it costs you if you get it wrong.

This book wasn't written to sell you anything, but I feel so strongly about this that if you are interested in learning more about my recruitment course, contact me on the email on the back cover and my team will send you more details.

POINTS TO CONSIDER:

- These days you need to market for the best people rather than advertise
- The marketing needs to sell the prospect on why they should apply
- There are many places to market for good people
- You want to have enough people apply that to you can choose from a good selection rather than choose from a bad batch of two or three
- An application pack is a great tool for finding out more from the applicants
- Consider outsourcing some parts of the process if you are very busy.

BUILDING TEAM CULTURE

Many good books have been written on building a great culture in businesses, and I've been privileged to have the opportunity to study and visit first hand some of the big companies that are touted as 'best practice' for amazing culture, such as Zappos (craziest place I've ever been), and Google - who wouldn't want to work there, with free healthy delicious meals every day from gourmet cafeterias, on site massage rooms and nap pods? But I always feel we are seeing the fun side of the culture that has been built in recent years with the trappings of wealth from a successful company rather than the real-world experience of how to build culture in a normal small or medium enterprise. However, there are still many ideas that can be gleaned from these big companies that are inexpensive to introduce into your own business.

When I owned the childcare centre, it was at a time when there was a shortage of qualified early childhood teachers in New Zealand, and on top of that, the government had decided to close some of the early childhood training institutions down and also increase the qualifications required to work in an early childhood centre. There was already a shortage of staff and it was getting worse! In fact, there was a joke that if a person applied for a job and had a degree or diploma in early childhood and had a heartbeat, then we should employ them.

I thought about this a lot and I figured the only way to combat the shortage was to build an awesome culture where people wanted to work at my centre rather than at another centre. I'm not saying I did a 100% perfect job of it either, as I was new to the industry and still learning, but I did build a culture where people would travel to work at my centre and drive right past several other competitors to get to there.

I guess we can all remember a workplace and a boss/leader/manager that was fantastic to work for. A place where you loved to come to work and did extra because it was enjoyable not because you felt you had to. If you are an employee reading this, and haven't had this experience, then it may be time to start looking for another job.

I had great experience once when I was an engineer in the dairy industry and seconded for a series of short term projects with a sub-contractor. My sub-contractor manager was someone who didn't 'Tell' me to do things, instead he would 'Coach' me. Each morning he would come into my office and the conversations would go like this: 'Morning Andrew, how is the project with the xxxxxx xxxxx going?' We would chat about the project, I would give any updates about problems or solutions for it and he would listen, and we would discuss ideas that would help with completing it. Then he would say something like, 'So have you heard about the water-hammer troubles with milk supply they are having at the Casein factory?' I would say 'yes' or 'no', and he would ask another question like: 'So in your opinion, what do you think could be causing the problem?' (Note: This is a great question as everyone wants to give their opinion.) I would usually reply with a theory in one or two directions and he would say 'Oh wow, that's a good theory, what do you think they need to do to fix it then?' By this time, I'm on a roll and I'm happy to divulge my ideas and solutions to the problem. Then he would say: 'Hey, I know you're busy but is there any chance you could pop your head in at Casein and have a quick look? Maybe you will be able to help them find a solution quickly?' You guessed it, I was more than happy to head to the Casein factory and save the day.

It took me a while to realize that he always knew what the problem was before he entered my office, and he also knew how to fix it, but he preferred to coach me into owning the solution and taking care of it. It was masterful and formed a fantastic culture to work in as it wasn't about the managers ego. I 100% enjoyed my time working for him, it was a shame when it come to an end and I had to go back to my original job and management structure, but I had learnt a lot about how a single person could produce an amazing culture to work in.

If you want to build a great culture in your own business, a culture where people are lining up to work for you, then I suggest you start by looking at yourself. Are you the type of leader that 'tells and yells' or do you coach and nurture your team? Are you the type of leader who Coaches your people? Is your mood consistent? Are you consistent across your team and treating everyone as an equal and equally? Do you show everyone on your team the same respect? Do you support their decision making even if sometimes they get it wrong?

All the fun things you can do to build team culture like an afternoons golfing or go-karting, meals out with partners, and so on are the easy part and won't create a wonderful workplace culture if you as the leader don't create that culture first.

CASE STUDY: CHANGING THE CULTURE

To give you an example of how much difference this can make, here's a case study of one of my long-term clients:

Steve owns a medium sized business with good revenue and profits and employs between 30 and 40 staff depending on the time of year. When I first met Steve, I noticed immediately that there was a negative environment, an almost toxic vibe to his business, I could see and feel it with his staff and his language when he talked about the team. He was averaging about 4 personal grievance law cases against him and his business every year, mainly because he would get so frustrated with the staff for 'Not doing what I tell them', that he would get angry and tell them to leave (that is the polite way of saying it). He wouldn't follow the protocol of how to dismiss an employee and hence the employee would engage a lawyer and another court case would begin, resulting in him losing because of the way he had conducted the dismissal. It cost him a lot of money each time too.

Immediately I said to him that we have to stop this happening and he may need to change how he is dealing with situations. This didn't go down too well but he agreed it was worth a try. We started with his recruitment system as he was constantly hiring new people and it looked to me he wasn't getting good quality candidates. His selection process also needed tuning as he was always stressed and would make hiring decisions quickly, feeling that 'they won't be here long anyway' (which was probably true)

The next thing we looked at was how he was communicating with his team, how he was speaking to them, emailing them, and how he was sending memos to them. I also worked with him on personality profiles, so he could understand himself and others much better, how best to interact, and what individuals needed in a work environment etc.

I conducted a survey with the team and got *a lot* of really honest feedback. I then met with the whole team for an afternoon to talk with them about what they would like the jobs to look like and what ideas did they have for improvements. We then went to work implementing their ideas and requests. It was a big ship we were attempting to turn around, degree by degree, and so it took some time to improve the culture, the structure, the roles and responsibilities, the communications between Steve and the team, and also within the team. But it was worth it. Steve now has a dedicated team, people lining up to work for him (he doesn't even need to advertise anymore) and job roles with structure, measurement and feedback. And of course, the feeling or vibe of the business is completely different and there have been no law suits for many years now.

I have repeated this process in many businesses, large and small, and had some people leave and take up another job 'At a place that is better for them and us'. Sometimes people don't want to change, they don't want the culture to improve and if that's the case, then they need to decide for themselves to move on. I've had key people leave in these situations, but it is always better for the owner, the business and the team culture in the long run, and everyone is replaceable. The funny thing is, it's always the people who were most disruptive or poor at their job that leave. Normally the good team members stay on and embrace the changes.

There are any other aspects to building culture such as developing the rules of the game or culture code for the business, developing a 'Why' or Vision and Mission Statement, designing a risk-taking supporting atmosphere etc., but what I've outlined above will give you a streetwise start.

ACCOUNTABILITY

As a business coach, much of what I do with my clients revolves around accountability, and it's a big subject, but here's a simple summary of some things I've observed:

Most business owners don't hold people accountable in their business, often choosing to do the uncompleted task themselves rather than use it as an example for improvement. This creates a frustrating never-ending cycle until the owner learns how to set tasks with a team member, resource them properly, coach, then follow up with consequences if the task isn't completed. Most people will say they want accountability but very few people actually do want to be held accountable. Basically, there are 3 types of accountability

1. Self-Accountability - make a promise to self and then try to keep it. New Year's resolutions are like this and the strategy can be very weak as most people don't stick to the plan. Some do though, and you will see this in their educational commitments, sports training, money saving etc.

2. Coaching Accountability - basically deciding on the task together, set a timeframe to do it and then I'll check how you've done. I use this type of accountability with my one-to-one clients and it is powerful for most people, especially if the accountability is positioned well.

3. Peer Accountability - setting a task and timeframe and committing to a group of peers that you will follow through. This is actually very powerful and immediately brings to mind a client of mine who commits to two other friends that he will join them at the gym Mondays, Wednesdays and Fridays. This is made even more powerful by a simple thing - there is a large monetary fine imposed if anyone of them doesn't turn up.

All three of these types of accountability can work, but for a business owner and the team you will really only use numbers 2 and 3 above. Firstly, coaching each person one-to-one in their role (or coaching the manager(s) in a larger business). Secondly, setting up team accountability; that is, having people commit to their team mates what they will achieve and by what date.

I'll emphasis it again though – there has to be consequences in both cases, otherwise people will just shrug their shoulders and psychologically think, 'Well nothing happened, I won't complete it next time either'. Please research and learn how to coach your people, I guarantee it will bring a world of easy people management to you.

POINTS TO CONSIDER:

- Cultural change starts with the owner and it isn't about the team going for an afternoon of paintballing or playing golf.

- An amazing culture will draw people to come and work for you, the better the culture, the higher the grade of applicants.

- It can take time and effort to change your business culture, but the rewards are worth it.

- Try coaching your team, rather than telling them what to do, it forces them to own the task(s) and actually makes it more enjoyable!

[7]

VISION, GOALS AND ACTIONS — WHAT DO YOU REALLY WANT TO ACHIEVE?

It's funny that this is almost the final chapter in my book yet it's my starting place with every business owner. What do you really want to achieve?

Some of the business owners I've met over many years say they have never set goals for their business, but I always find this ironic, as they have built some kind of business with a revenue generated from customers and a product or service they sell. Somewhere along the way they must have set at least some targets or goals, maybe at least like, 'Making enough money to pay the bills'.

The truth is, that every business owner has set some kind of goals to get where they are currently, and the exciting news is, if you put some focus on where you are going next, then there's a high chance you might arrive there!

I use a process developed by ActionCOACH called an 'Alignment Process' to establish:

a). Where is the business right now, what is working, what is not working?
b). Where does the owner want to take the business in the future?
c). What are the strategies and tactics that need to be learned and applied, tested and measured to achieve this?
d). Is the business actually capable of generating the results the owner is looking for?
e). Is the owner up to the challenge and coachable?

From this process we work though the owners *Vision* and *Goals* and then the *Projects* and *Actions* that need to be taken in order to achieve the *Objectives*.

It is a very powerful process and the results can be then used to produce an Alignment Plan, which is a little like a business plan, but in my mind anyway, a lot more streetwise.

See the image on the following page:

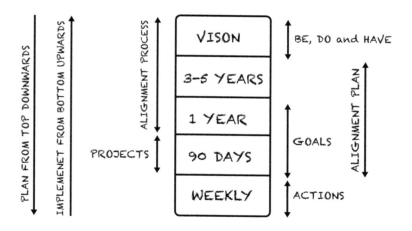

In the diagram above, you can see a ladder model with:
- Weekly – Actions that need to be taken weekly.
- 90 days – Projects that are targeted for completion within a 90 day or three month time period.
- 1 year – 1 year goals that the 90 day projects feed into.
- 3-5 years – 3-5 year goals, maybe 10 years if you want to think further out, the yearly goals feed into these larger 3-5 year goals.
- Vision – the vision of the ultimate achievements you have in mind for your business and yourself, maybe even a legacy.

Down the sides of the ladder you can see where the Alignment Process and Alignment Plan fit in, and also the actions, projects and goals. It's amazing when a business owner is coached on implementing with this model, how small weekly actions at the bottom, can, and do, produce BIG results at the top of the ladder.

I've read a lot of business plans from business owners who are usually forced into writing one when they want to gain finance for their business. Often, I find them covered in dust on top of a filling cabinet or tucked away in a drawer. And most often, if they had actually implemented everything that is detailed, they would have a great looking business.

So, there is a disconnect between writing and having a plan and actually following though and implementing on it. If this sounds familiar, don't despair as I know 100% for sure that business coaching with a great coach really works and will help you follow though to achieve what you desire. But only if you are committed.

[8]

CHOOSING YOUR TRUSTED ADVISORS BOARD

One thing I've found in common with very successful business owners, is they have a circle or 'board' of trusted advisors, people they have sought out to guide and help them as they build their business. A good bank manager, a good employment lawyer, a good general solicitor, a great accountant and a great coach or mentor. These are people you can quickly text, email or talk to when you have a short-term crisis, some medium-term ideas or, are planning for the distant future.

I would say approximately 40% of the business owners I've met aren't happy with some of the advisors they have chosen. My advice is to brainstorm what you need from each one of these people and then interview a few that have been recommended, don't just take the first one that contacts you.

Your choice of business coach or mentor is one of the most crucial as you will probably be interacting with him/her the most, so tread carefully - the industry is unregulated and continues to grow with people claiming they are the best coach/mentor when all they have done is read a few books and printed a set of business cards. Many have never even owned a business of their own! Be careful of the words 'guru' 'ninja' and 'wizard' in their job title, these are normally buzzwords people throw around to give the impression they are an expert but maybe aren't, check them out thoroughly - your business depends on it!

CONCLUSION

A few years ago, my wife and I decided we wanted to custom design our own home and so we visited show home after show home looking at designs, layouts, features and materials used. Every show home we visited seemed to have at least one detail or feature that was different to the others. It could be the LED lighting that was installed under the kitchen bench, or the way the basin was recessed into the wall, or the negative detailing along the top of the cupboards and so on. This got me thinking, what if we were to incorporate many of the cool things we had noticed into our own house? So that's what we endeavored to do and now we enjoy many people commenting on features in our home.

I think business improvement is a little like this too, if you look across at another business and really like something they are doing with customer service, or the thankyou cards they send out, or their accounts receivable system or their employment methods, then why not take the idea and implement it into your own business, (I'm not taking about directly copying a competitor here). Many small improvements in every area of your business will give you a **BIG** differentiation against your competitors and make it far easier to market your products and services.

I hope you have enjoyed the ideas, strategies and stories in this book and I hope you will go to work and implement things you may have learnt. For me business is a pure joy and I can't imagine doing anything else other than working one-to-one with business owners, working with teams, sitting on boards, training teams or other business coaches, or keynote speaking at conferences around the world.

I also hope that you now have more of an understanding of the power small changes can have in your business, and you will endeavor to implement some of the things I have outlined in this book. My plan is to write several books to include marketing, financial analysis, tax reduction, etc. If you want to be notified when these books come out, then connect with my team and they'll put you on the list.

If you are looking to *Be more, Do more*, and *Have more* in your business and life, then also reach out to my team at: *admin@smallchangesbigresults.global* and we'll have a conversation to see if or how we can help you.

If you're looking for a world proven, fun and engaging speaker with a powerful business message then again, connect with my team and we'll see if we can help. It's been an honor to finally organize, collate and put some of my thoughts onto paper for you.

See you on the other side!

Andrew

TESTIMONIALS

Andrew is constantly developing his skills, and when it comes to coaching and presenting, he does a terrific job making the complicated simple, which is always appreciated. Secondly, he lives and leads by example. I don't think he would ever ask you to do something that he hasn't already done himself. With all the success he has achieved in life to date, Andrew has remained humble and giving. If you're looking to take your business to a new level of professionalism and success, I highly recommend you speak with Andrew... it will be worth it. *Vince Fowler, Calgary, Canada*

It has been a pleasure the last few years working with Andrew. He has a special way on how he engages people when it comes to helping them fulfil their dreams and grow their business. I find Andrews approach fresh, laser-focused and creative. He has amazing energy and passion for what he does and truly cares about the business owners and their business. I would definitely recommend Andrew as a presenter, speaker, facilitator and coach. *Angie Fairbanks, Las Vegas Nevada*

Andrew gets what it takes to train and mentor business people. He has a unique ability to relate and communicate 'Business' and 'Life' principles and concepts in simple terms. With his passion for what he does, I would happily recommend Andrew as both a Coach and Mentor. *Phil Badura, Albury Wodonga, Australia*

Andrew Johnston is a proven business coach. He doesn't tell you theories... He'll show you what he's achieved. This is why he gets awesome results with his clients. Oh, and if you want Andrew to facilitate a group session for you, expect fun and learnings. Andrew has a great way to relate with people at all levels. This is what makes him a great facilitator. On the personal front, he has been a great friend to me who has been a mentor and a person who encourages me onwards towards my dreams. *Cynthia Wihardja, Jakarta, Indonesia*

I first met Andrew Johnston at a Coaching conference in January 2012. Andrew is one of those character rich people who always brings out the best in others - it could be as simple as a thoughtful compliment or lending an ear and sharing some timely advice. I've known Andrew for about 7 years, have participated in his seminars and workshops and have found that he has a great ability to take complex situations and break them down into simple steps that virtually anyone can implement. When Andrew is talking, I recommend you listen! *Bill Gilliland, Asheville, North Carolina, USA*

Andrew has an in-depth knowledge and ability of bringing people and business to their maximum potential. With a pleasant and relaxed style Andrew is a brilliant presenter either on line or in person. *Denis Buckley, Dublin, Ireland*

Andrew added value to my business with regards to online and communication strategies to my database. He is a wealth of knowledge in this area and I found his guidance very valuable. His encouragement and abundant approach to sharing his tools of trade and ideas was awesome! *Charmian Campbell, Brisbane, Australia*

Andrew is a highly successful business coach trainer and growth coach particularly for those wanting to grow their business to the next level. Andrew has vast experience in getting businesses on track and expanding themselves emotionally to be better coaches for their clients whether this is one on one or at group coach training events. Andrew also makes it fun and is able to mix in all circles and cultures. Andrew's programs are absolutely first class, he is super creative, confident and generous in sharing an absolute gold mine of detailed ways we can grow our businesses, increase their business profits and free up our time. *Mark Blume, Orange, Australia*

Andrew has a huge wealth of experience, but he clearly remembers what it's like to be a rookie. He patiently but energetically and with great humor and fun takes you through a whole host of useful, practical strategies and tools with real examples of the difference each has made to his own clients. He seems to have a bag of solutions for everything and everyone! I now have a mass of brilliant ideas that I'm implementing myself. *Ros Jones, Scarborough, North Yorkshire, U.K.*

Andrew's webinar and coaching programs have been invaluable to me in growing and improving my business. The strategies he teaches enabled me to provide immediate value to my clients and contributed immensely to my reputation in business. I have been able to employ new strategies every week as a result of the straight-forward, easy to implement way Andrew outlines each and every one. Thanks Andrew. *Dave Lakin, Huntsville, Alabama*

Your programs are a home run. Every bit of the content is easy to follow and apply immediately to my clients and prospects. Absolutely no doubt about getting a fantastic return on my investment to enroll. I am always amazed at your ability to explain ways to improve businesses so simply. While most coaches and trainers struggle to teach practical strategy you always seem to make it easy. Thank you for everything you do. *Terry Elton, Portland, Oregon, USA*

Just a quick note to thank you for the 'Increase your Profitability' program conducted over the last three months. The tips and tricks you gave to us to improve our businesses were relevant and the examples given made the process of understanding how to implement them EASY! I would recommend this training for anyone who is coaching businesses and highly recommend Andrew Johnston as a 1-2-1 coach, presenter and facilitator of seminars and webinars. Thanks again for everything and I look forward to the new series on marketing and sales and I'm sure it will be as informative and helpful as the previous programs. *Luke Whitton, Orange, Australia*

Are you looking for highly practical tips for gaining clients and improving your business? Let Andrew Johnston help you. I have participated in several of Andrew's programs and can tell you Andrew gives you fantastic, practical ideas that he has used personally and will show you exactly how he applied the strategy/tactic. You will get a good return on your investment! *Mark Samuel, Plymouth Meeting, Pennsylvania, USA*

I found that Andrew's webinar programs are packed with practical advice on how to promote my business and to convert and keep clients. They have helped me to increase my marketing activity to generate and convert more leads. *Kevin O'Keeffe, Cork, Ireland*

ABOUT THE AUTHOR

Andrew's official working life started out in 1986 when he took on a fitter/turner apprenticeship at the Carter Holt Harvey Paper Mill in Mataura, Southland, New Zealand. As a child he grew up on a sheep farm in the deep south of New Zealand. Like many farmers children, he was heavily involved in helping with farm work from an early age, from mustering stock, shifting electric fences, shearing, lambing, hay and silage making, working the land for winter crops, or working in his fathers' workshop maintaining and repairing machinery.

From this experience a strong work ethic was instilled in him and continues to this day. He has built several businesses from nothing and has revitalized others. With the knowledge and experience he had gained over many years, he was presented the idea and opportunity to become a business coach to teach others what he had learnt.

He has now been a highly successful business coach with a global client list, since 2005. Coach, key-note speaker, presenter and global coach trainer, Andrew has a vast knowledge of practical streetwise business strategies that can transform a business. His area of passion is helping small to medium sized business owners. Coaching the owner one-on-one, mentoring individuals in a business or working with the team.

Andrew's coaching methods and knowledge have changed the lives of hundreds of business owners, their families and their teams.

Lightning Source UK Ltd.
Milton Keynes UK
UKHW020018111220
374921UK00012B/2698